Cases and Materials on
The Law of the European Union

Authors

Daryll Bewick

Chris Garside

Alex Lawson

Consultant Editor

Glenn Robinson

First edition July 2010

Third edition August 2012

Published ISBN 9781 4453 9954 6

Previous ISBN 9781 4453 8409 2

British Library Cataloguing-in-Publication Data
A catalogue record for this book is available
from the British Library

Published by
BPP Learning Media Ltd
BPP House, Aldine Place
London W12 8AA
www.bpp.com/learningmedia

Printed in the United Kingdom by Polestar
Wheatons

Polestar Wheatons
Hennock Road
Marsh Barton
Exeter
EX2 8RP

Contents

Index of Cases

A

B

C

D

E

F

G

H

I

J

K

L

M

N

P

R

S

T

U

V

Introduction

The European Union

The European Union has not always been known by that name. The original grouping was known as the European Economic Community (EEC) reflecting its economic focus. This later became known as the European Community, to reflect a broader purpose and role of the Community. In the 1992 Maastricht Treaty the European Union was created, but the European Community remained as one of the three pillars which made up the Union. However, following the coming into force of the Lisbon Treaty, the pillar system was collapsed and now all 'European' law is created under the auspice of the European Union. In this Casebook we will refer throughout only to the European Union or EU. But please not that depending on what period the case actually comes from the judgment may refer to either the European Economic Community (EEC) or the European Community (EC).

The Treaties

The original Treaty setting up the European Economic Community was the Treaty of Rome. Throughout this Casebook we will refer to 'the Treaty' or to Articles, without specific reference to The Treaty of Rome. However, when such reference is made it is to the Treaty of Rome.

Articles

There have been many Treaties signed by the members of the EU since the Treaty of Rome. A large number of these subsequent Treaties have amended the Treaty of Rome. A consequence of this has been that the original Treaty has been renumbered several times. This means that the Articles mentioned in old case law rarely match up to where the corresponding Article can be found in the Treaty of Rome as amended. Throughout this work we will refer to the current numbering. However, where Articles are referred to in a particular judgment, in order to assist you the old numbering will also be set out. So, for instance, legislation will be cited as: Arts 52 (ex Art 49), Art 54 (ex Art 48) and Art 56 (ex Art 59). This means that the current Arts which can be found in the statutory material are 52, 54 and 56.

1

Constitutional and Administrative Law of the EU

Topic List

Alex Lawson

Introduction

The European Union has evolved from humble inter-governmental beginnings to become a truly supra-national organisation. As such, it has developed a corpus of constitutional and administrative law to regulate the interaction of the various institutions. Most of the case law in this area is in the field of administrative law, with constitutional law being still somewhat regulated at the inter-governmental level. Few disputes in this area get to court as states do not like to be seen to appear before the European Court of Justice for such basic violations, and will tend to resolve the matters at issue before they get to such an advanced stage.

1 Constitutional Law

This subject has seen only one major case, but it showcases many of the different legal principles that can be considered by the ECJ in their consideration of the legality of the activities (in this case legislative) of Union institutions.

United Kingdom of Great Britain and Northern Ireland v Council of the European Union, Case C-84/94 [1996] 3 CMLR 671

Panel: Rodríguez Iglesias P; Mancini, Moitinho de Almeida (Rapporteur), Murray and Sevón PPC; Kakouris, Kapteyn, Gulmann, Edward, Puissochet, Hirsch, Jann and Ragnemalm JJ. Mr Philippe Léger, Advocate-General

Legislation: Art 118 (now repealed)

Facts: This case concerned the judicial enforcement of the principle of 'subsidiarity'. The UK's position was that the principle militated against the creation of a working time directive, on the broad grounds that the issue could be adequately addressed by action by the Member States (the four specific reasons cited for this were that the legal basis of the directive was defective, proportionality had been ignored, the directive constituted misuse of powers and infringement of essential procedural requirements). The Court of Justice's approach seems to have rendered the concept of subsidiarity essentially non-justiciable. The case is useful in that it constitutes one of the few practical applications of fundamental judicial principles within the topic of constitutional law. The Article in the case has now been repealed following the adoption of the Lisbon Treaty.

> JUDGMENT
>
> 1 By application lodged at the Court Registry on 8 March 1994, the United Kingdom of Great Britain and Northern Ireland brought an action under Article 173 of the EC Treaty for the annulment of Council Directive 93/104/EC of 23 November 1993 concerning certain aspects of the organization of working time (OJ 1993 L 307, p. 18, hereinafter "the directive") and, in the alternative, of Article 4, the first and second sentences of Article 5, Article 6(2) and Article 7 of the directive.
>
> 2 The directive was adopted on the basis of Article 118a of the Treaty, which provides as follows:

"(1). Member States shall pay particular attention to encouraging improvements, especially in the working environment, as regards the health and safety of workers, and shall set as their objective the harmonization of conditions in this area, while maintaining the improvements made.

(2). In order to help achieve the objective laid down in the first paragraph, the Council, acting in accordance with the procedure referred to in Article 189c and after consulting the Economic and Social Committee, shall adopt by means of directives minimum requirements for gradual implementation, having regard to the conditions and technical rules obtaining in each of the Member States.

Such directives shall avoid imposing administrative, financial and legal constraints in a way which would hold back the creation and development of small and medium-sized undertakings.

(3). The provisions adopted pursuant to this article shall not prevent any Member State from maintaining or introducing more stringent measures for the protection of working conditions compatible with this Treaty."

3 The directive, in accordance with Article 1 thereof, lays down minimum health and safety requirements for the organization of working time, and applies to all sectors of activity, both public and private, within the meaning of Article 2 of Council Directive 89/391/EEC of 12 June 1989 on the introduction of measures to encourage improvements in the safety and health of workers at work (OJ 1989 L 183, p. 1), with the exception of air, rail, road, sea, inland waterway and lake transport, sea fishing, other work at sea and the activities of doctors in training. ...

[The court set out the directive and continued:]

7 Member States are also to take measures to ensure that an employer who regularly uses night workers brings that information to the attention of the competent authorities if they so request (Article 11). Finally, where work is organized according to a certain pattern, employers are to take account of the general principle of adapting work to the worker, with a view, in particular, to alleviating monotonous work and work at a predetermined work-rate, depending on the type of activity, and also of health and safety requirements (Article 13).

8 Section IV of the directive contains miscellaneous provisions. Article 14 provides that the directive is not to apply where there are other more specific Community provisions concerning certain occupations or occupational activities. Article 15 provides that Member States may apply, or permit the application of, provisions which are more favourable than those contained in the directive. Article 16 empowers Member States to lay down reference periods for the application of the provisions on the weekly rest period, maximum weekly working time and the length of night work. Finally, Article 17 lists the derogations, which may be made from certain provisions, while Article 18 lays down various periods for transposition of the directive into national law.

Reason One

The plea that the legal base of the directive is defective

10 The applicant contends that the directive should have been adopted on the basis of Article 100 of the EC Treaty, or Article 235 of the Treaty, which require unanimity within the Council.

The scope of Article 118a

11 The applicant observes in the first place that, because Article 118a of the Treaty must be regarded as an exception to Article 100 - which, pursuant to Article 100a(2), is the article that covers provisions "relating to the rights and interests of employed persons" - it must be strictly interpreted.

12 As the Court pointed out in Opinion 2/91 of 19 March 1993 ([1993] ECR I-1061, paragraph 17), Article 118a confers upon the Community internal legislative competence in the area of social policy. The existence of other provisions in the Treaty does not have the effect of restricting the scope of Article 118a. Appearing as it does in the chapter of the Treaty which deals with "Social Provisions", Article 118a relates only to measures concerning the protection of the health and safety of workers. It therefore constitutes a more specific rule than Articles 100 and 100a. That interpretation is confirmed by the actual wording of Article 100a (1) itself, which states that its provisions are to apply "save where otherwise provided in this Treaty". The applicant's argument cannot therefore be accepted.

13 Second, referring to the actual wording of Article 118a, the applicant argues first that that provision permits the adoption only of directives which have a genuine and objective link to the "health and safety" of workers. That does not apply to measures concerning, in particular, weekly working time, paid annual leave and rest periods, whose connection with the health and safety of workers is too tenuous. That interpretation is borne out by the expression "working environment" used in Article 118a, which implies that directives based on that provision must be concerned only with physical conditions and risks at the workplace.

14 In that respect, it should be noted that Article 118a(2), read in conjunction with Article 118a(1), empowers the Council to adopt, by means of directives, minimum requirements for gradual implementation, having regard to the conditions and technical rules obtaining in each of the Member States, with a view to "encouraging improvements, especially in the working environment, as regards the health and safety of workers" by harmonizing conditions in this area, while maintaining the improvements made.

15 There is nothing in the wording of Article 118a to indicate that the concepts of "working environment", "safety" and "health" as used in that provision should, in the absence of other indications, be interpreted restrictively, and not as embracing all factors, physical or otherwise, capable of affecting the health and safety of the worker in his working environment, including in particular certain aspects of the organization of working time. On the contrary, the words "especially in the working environment" militate in favour of a broad interpretation of the powers which Article 118a confers

upon the Council for the protection of the health and safety of workers. Moreover, such an interpretation of the words "safety" and "health" derives support in particular from the preamble to the Constitution of the World Health Organization to which all the Member States belong. Health is there defined as a state of complete physical, mental and social well-being that does not consist only in the absence of illness or infirmity.

16 The applicant further argues that under Article 118a(2) the Council may adopt only "minimum requirements" for gradual implementation, having regard to the conditions and technical rules obtaining in the Member States. That provision therefore empowers the Council to adopt harmonization measures only at a level acceptable to all Member States and constituting a minimum benchmark.

17 In conferring on the Council power to lay down minimum requirements, Article 118a does not prejudge the extent of the action which that institution may consider necessary in order to carry out the task which the provision in question expressly assigns to it - namely, to work in favour of improved conditions, as regards the health and safety of workers, while maintaining the improvements made. The significance of the expression "minimum requirements" in Article 118a is simply, as indeed Article 118a(3) confirms, that the provision authorizes Member States to adopt more stringent measures than those which form the subject-matter of Community action (see, in particular, Opinion 2/91, cited above, paragraph 18).

18 Third, the applicant argues that, in the light of previous directives based on Article 118a, that provision does not authorize the Council to adopt directives, such as that in dispute here, which deal with the question of health and safety in a generalized, unspecific and unscientific manner. Thus, Directive 89/391 established a risk assessment procedure designed to pinpoint specific areas in which action was required to safeguard the health and safety of workers. Similarly, the other directives based on Article 118a fall into two categories, namely "individual" directives within the meaning of Article 16 of Directive 89/391 (concerning, in particular, the provision of safety and health signs at work or the regulation of risks connected with exposure to carcinogens), and directives which, whilst not based on Directive 89/391, clearly focus upon a specific health or safety problem in a specific situation.

19 It is settled case-law that what is merely Council practice cannot derogate from the rules laid down in the Treaty, and cannot therefore create a precedent binding on the Community institutions with regard to the correct legal basis (see, in particular, Case 68/86 *United Kingdom v Council* [1988] ECR 855, paragraph 24, and Case C-271/94 *Parliament v Council* [1996] ECR I-1705, paragraph 24). Moreover, measures having a general scope have been adopted on the basis of Article 118a of the Treaty, as is demonstrated in particular by Council Directive 89/654/EEC of 30 November 1989 concerning the minimum safety and health requirements for the workplace (first individual directive within the meaning of Article 16(1) of Directive 89/391/EEC) (OJ 1989 L 393, p. 1).

20 Furthermore, there is no support in the wording of Article 118a for the argument that Community action should be restricted to specific measures applicable to given groups of workers in particular situations, whilst measures for wider purposes should be

adopted on the basis of Article 100 of the Treaty. Article 118a refers to "workers" generally and states that the objective which it pursues is to be achieved by the harmonization of "conditions" in general existing in the area of the health and safety of those workers.

21 In addition, the delimitation of the respective fields of application of Articles 100 and 100a, on the one hand, and Article 118a, on the other, rests not upon a distinction between the possibility of adopting general measures in the former case and particular measures in the latter, but upon the principal aim of the measure envisaged.

22 It follows that, where the principal aim of the measure in question is the protection of the health and safety of workers, Article 118a must be used, albeit such a measure may have ancillary effects on the establishment and functioning of the internal market (see, in particular, *Parliament v Council*, cited above, paragraph 32).

23 Finally, it is to be remembered that it is not the function of the Court to review the expediency of measures adopted by the legislature. The review exercised under Article 173 must be limited to the legality of the disputed measure.

24 It is in the light of those considerations that the Court must examine whether the directive was properly adopted on the basis of Article 118a of the Treaty.

Clearly the key issue here is how the court will examine the relationship between the Commission and the Member State.

The choice of legal basis for the directive

25 As part of the system of Community competence, the choice of the legal basis for a measure must be based on objective factors, which are amenable to judicial review (see, in particular, Case 45/86 *Commission v Council* [1987] ECR 1493, paragraph 11). Those factors include, in particular, the aim and content of the measure (see, in particular, Case C-300/89 *Commission v Council* [1991] ECR I-2867, paragraph 10).

26 As regards the aim of the directive, the applicant argues that it represents a continuation of the Community's earlier thinking and of a series of earlier initiatives at Community level concerned with the organization of working time in the interests of job creation and reduced unemployment. It is in reality a measure concerned with the overall improvement of the living and working conditions of employees and with their general protection, and is so broad in its scope and coverage as to be capable of classification as a social policy measure, for the adoption of which other legal bases exist.

27 It is to be noted in that respect that, according to the sixth recital in its preamble, the directive constitutes a practical contribution towards creating the social dimension of the internal market. However, it does not follow from the fact that the directive falls within the scope of Community social policy that it cannot properly be based on Article 118a, so long as it contributes to encouraging improvements as regards the health and safety of workers. Indeed, Article 118a forms part of Chapter 1, headed "Social Provisions", of Title VIII of the Treaty, which deals in particular with "Social Policy". This

led the Court to conclude that that provision conferred on the Community internal legislative competence in the area of social policy (Opinion 2/91, cited above, paragraph 17).

28 Furthermore, as the Advocate General has demonstrated in points 85 to 90 of his Opinion, the organization of working time is not necessarily conceived as an instrument of employment policy. In this case, the fifth recital in the preamble to the directive states that the improvement of workers' safety, hygiene and health at work is an objective which should not be subordinated to "purely economic considerations". Were the organization of working time to be viewed as a means of combating unemployment, a number of economic factors would have to be taken into account, such as, for example, its impact on the productivity of undertakings and on workers' salaries.

29 The approach taken by the directive, viewing the organization of working time essentially in terms of the favourable impact it may have on the health and safety of workers, is apparent from several recitals in its preamble. Thus, for example, the eighth recital states that, in order to ensure the safety and health of Community workers, they must be granted minimum rest periods and adequate breaks and that it is also necessary in that context to place a maximum limit on weekly working hours. In addition, the eleventh recital states that "research has shown that... long periods of night work can be detrimental to the health of workers and can endanger safety at the workplace", while the fifteenth recital states that specific working conditions may have detrimental effects on the safety and health of workers and that the organization of work according to a certain pattern must take account of the general principle of adapting work to the worker.

30 While, in the light of those considerations, it cannot be excluded that the directive may affect employment, that is clearly not its essential objective.

31 As regards the content of the directive, the applicant argues that the connection between the measures it lays down, on the one hand, and health and safety, on the other, is too tenuous for the directive to be based on Article 118a of the Treaty.

32 In that respect, it argues that no adequate scientific evidence exists to justify the imposition of a general requirement to provide for breaks where the working day is longer than six hours (Article 4), a general requirement to provide for a minimum uninterrupted weekly rest period of twenty-four hours in addition to the usual eleven hours' daily rest (Article 5, first sentence), a requirement that the minimum rest period must, in principle, include Sunday (Article 5, second sentence), a general requirement to ensure that the average working time for each seven-day period, including overtime, does not exceed forty-eight hours (Article 6(2)), and a general requirement that every worker is to have a minimum of four weeks' paid annual leave (Article 7).

33 The applicant points out in that connection that Directive 89/391 provides for employers to carry out assessments to evaluate specific risks to the health and safety of workers, taking into account the nature of the activities of the undertaking. The risk assessment procedure laid down by Directive 89/391 could not apply to the restrictions on working time contained in Section II of the contested directive (and is

applicable only to a very limited extent in Section III), the provisions in question being quite simply mandatory and leaving no scope for such an assessment in order to determine whether they are to apply.

34 The applicant maintains, moreover, that unlike other provisions based on Article 118a of the Treaty, the contested measures were not referred to the Advisory Committee on Safety, Hygiene and Health Protection at Work for an opinion (on the role of such committees, it cites Case C-212/91 *Angelopharm* [1994] ECR I-171, paragraphs 31 and 32). Although consultation of that committee is not expressly provided for in cases such as this, the fact that the Council did not call on the Commission to undertake such consultation casts further doubt on the link between the directive and the health and safety of workers.

35 Finally, in the applicant's view, contrary to the requirements of Article 118a(2), the provisions of the directive do not constitute "minimum requirements for gradual implementation, having regard to the conditions and technical rules obtaining in each of the Member States" and do not take account of their effects on "the creation and development of small and medium-sized undertakings".

36 In order to deal with those arguments, a distinction must be drawn between the second sentence of Article 5 of the directive and its other provisions.

37 As to the second sentence of Article 5, whilst the question whether to include Sunday in the weekly rest period is ultimately left to the assessment of Member States, having regard, in particular, to the diversity of cultural, ethnic and religious factors in those States (second sentence of Article 5, read in conjunction with the tenth recital), the fact remains that the Council has failed to explain why Sunday, as a weekly rest day, is more closely connected with the health and safety of workers than any other day of the week. In those circumstances, the applicant's alternative claim must be upheld and the second sentence of Article 5, which is severable from the other provisions of the directive, must be annulled.

38 The other measures laid down by the directive, which refer to minimum rest periods, length of work, night work, shift work and the pattern of work, relate to the "working environment" and reflect concern for the protection of "the health and safety of workers". The scope of those terms has been explained in paragraph 15 of this judgment. Moreover, as the Belgian Government has pointed out, the evolution of social legislation at both national and international level confirms the existence of a link between measures relating to working time and the health and safety of workers.

39 Legislative action by the Community, particularly in the field of social policy, cannot be limited exclusively to circumstances where the justification for such action is scientifically demonstrated (see points 165 to 167 of the Advocate General's Opinion).

40 Similarly, the applicant's argument that the directive precludes any assessment of the risks involved for certain workers or for those working in a particular sector cannot be regarded as well founded. The Community legislature did take certain special situations into account, as is demonstrated by Article 1 of the directive, which excludes certain sectors or activities from its scope by Article 14, which excludes occupations and occupational activities where more specific Community provisions apply and by

Article 17(1) and (2) which allow derogations from Articles 3, 4, 5, 6 and 8 in respect of certain groups of workers or certain sectors of activity (see points 114 to 117 of the Advocate General' s Opinion).

41 It is true that the Council did not consult the Advisory Committee on Safety, Hygiene and Health Protection at Work established by Council Decision 74/325/EEC of 27 June 1974 (OJ 1974 L 185, p. 15) with regard to the measures envisaged by the directive. However, under Article 2(1) of that decision, such consultation is intended only "[to assist] the Commission in the preparation and implementation of activities in the fields of safety, hygiene and health protection at work", and does not therefore constitute a condition precedent for action by the Council. In those circumstances, failure to consult that committee cannot be relied on to cast doubt on the link between the measures laid down by the directive and the protection of the health and safety of workers.

42 Furthermore, the provisions of the directive are "minimum requirements" within the meaning of Article 118a of the Treaty. Whilst ensuring a certain level of protection for workers, the directive authorizes Member States in Article 15 to apply, or facilitate the application of, measures which are more favourable to the protection of the health and safety of workers, thereby guaranteeing them a more stringent level of protection, in accordance with Article 118a(3). Similarly, Article 18(3) of the directive states that, whilst Member States may provide for different measures in the field of working time, subject to compliance with the minimum requirements it lays down, implementation of the directive does not constitute valid grounds for reducing the general level of protection afforded to workers.

43 The measures laid down by the directive are also, in accordance with Article 118a, "for gradual implementation, having regard to the conditions and technical rules obtaining in each of the Member States". In the first place, it is not in dispute that legislation in all the Member States includes measures on the organization of working time. Furthermore, Article 18 of the directive authorizes Member States, subject to certain conditions, not to apply, after the expiry of the time-limit for implementing the directive (23 November 1996), the provisions of Article 6 on weekly working time or, for a three-year transitional period, the provisions of Article 7 on paid annual leave, which may during that period be limited to three weeks.

44 Finally, the directive has taken account of the effects which the organization of working time for which it provides may have on small and medium-sized undertakings. Thus, the second recital in the preamble to the directive refers to the overriding requirement not to hold back the development of such undertakings. Moreover, as the Court held in its judgment in Case C-189/91 *Kirsammer-Hack v Sidal* [1993] ECR I-6185, paragraph 34, by providing that directives adopted in the field of health and safety of workers are to avoid imposing administrative, financial and legal constraints such as to hold back the creation and development of small and medium-sized undertakings, the second sentence of Article 118a(2) indicates that such undertakings may be the subject of special economic measures. Contrary to the view taken by the applicant, however, that provision does not prevent those undertakings from being subject to binding measures.

45 Since it is clear from the above considerations that, in terms of its aim and content, the directive has as its principal objective the protection of the health and safety of workers by the imposition of minimum requirements for gradual implementation, neither Article 100 nor Article 100a could have constituted the appropriate legal basis for its adoption.

46 The applicant further maintains that the Community legislature neither fully considered nor adequately demonstrated whether there were transnational aspects which could not be satisfactorily regulated by national measures, whether such measures would conflict with the requirements of the EC Treaty or significantly damage the interests of Member States or, finally, whether action at Community level would provide clear benefits compared with action at national level. In its submission, Article 118a should be interpreted in the light of the principle of subsidiarity, which does not allow adoption of a directive in such wide and prescriptive terms as the contested directive, given that the extent and the nature of legislative regulation of working time vary very widely between Member States. The applicant explains in this context, however, that it does not rely upon infringement of the principle of subsidiarity as a separate plea.

47 In that respect, it should be noted that it is the responsibility of the Council, under Article 118a, to adopt minimum requirements so as to contribute, through harmonization, to achieving the objective of raising the level of health and safety protection of workers which, in terms of Article 118a(1), is primarily the responsibility of the Member States. Once the Council has found that it is necessary to improve the existing level of protection as regards the health and safety of workers and to harmonize the conditions in this area while maintaining the improvements made, achievement of that objective through the imposition of minimum requirements necessarily presupposes Community-wide action, which otherwise, as in this case, leaves the enactment of the detailed implementing provisions required largely to the Member States. The argument that the Council could not properly adopt measures as general and mandatory as those forming the subject-matter of the directive will be examined below in the context of the plea alleging infringement of the principle of proportionality.

48 Finally, as regards Article 235 of the Treaty, it is sufficient to point to the Court's case-law, which holds that that article may be used as the legal basis for a measure only where no other Treaty provision confers on the Community institutions the necessary power to adopt it (see, in particular, Parliament v Council, cited above, paragraph 13).

49 It must therefore be held that the directive was properly adopted on the basis of Article 118a, save for the second sentence of Article 5, which must accordingly be annulled.

Again, note how the relationship of the Member State to the Community is being assessed.

Reason Two

The plea of breach of the principle of proportionality

50 The applicant points out that the Council may adopt on the basis of Article 118a of the Treaty only "minimum requirements for gradual implementation, having regard to the conditions and technical rules obtaining in each of the Member States", and that those requirements must avoid "imposing administrative, financial and legal constraints in a way which would hold back the creation and development of small and medium-sized undertakings". In its submission, four broad principles are relevant in assessing whether or not the requirements imposed by the contested directive are minimum requirements within the meaning of Article 118a.

51 First, it argues, not all measures which may "improve" the level of health and safety protection of workers constitute minimum requirements. In particular, those consisting in global reductions in working time or global increases in rest periods, whilst having a certain beneficial effect on the health or safety of workers, do not constitute "minimum requirements" within the meaning of Article 118a.

52 Second, a provision cannot be regarded as a "minimum requirement" if the level of health and safety protection of workers which it establishes can be attained by measures that are less restrictive and involve fewer obstacles to the competitiveness of industry and the earning capacity of individuals. In the applicant's submission, neither the Commission's proposals nor the directive provide any explanation as to why the desired level of protection could not have been achieved by less restrictive measures, such as, for example, the use of risk assessments if working hours exceeded particular norms.

53 Third, the conclusion that the measures envisaged will in fact improve the level of health or safety protection of workers must be based on reasonable grounds. In its view, the present state of scientific research in the area concerned falls far short of justifying the contested measures.

54 Fourth, a measure will be proportionate only if it is consistent with the principle of subsidiarity. The applicant argues that it is for the Community institutions to demonstrate that the aims of the directive could better be achieved at Community level than by action on the part of the Member States. There has been no such demonstration in this case.

55 The argument of non-compliance with the principle of subsidiarity can be rejected at the outset. It is said that the Community legislature has not established that the aims of the directive would be better served at Community level than at national level. But that argument, as so formulated, really concerns the need for Community action, which has already been examined in paragraph 47 of this judgment.

56 Furthermore, as is clear from paragraph 17 of this judgment, the applicant bases its argument on a conception of "minimum requirements" which differs from that in Article 118a. That provision does not limit Community action to the lowest common denominator, or even to the lowest level of protection established by the various

Member States, but means that Member States are free to provide a level of protection more stringent than that resulting from Community law, high as it may be.

57 As regards the principle of proportionality, the Court has held that, in order to establish whether a provision of Community law complies with that principle, it must be ascertained whether the means which it employs are suitable for the purpose of achieving the desired objective and whether they do not go beyond what is necessary to achieve it (see, in particular, Case C-426/93 Germany v Council [1995] ECR I-3723, paragraph 42).

 Alert

58 As to judicial review of those conditions, however, the Council must be allowed a wide discretion in an area which, as here, involves the legislature in making social policy choices and requires it to carry out complex assessments. Judicial review of the exercise of that discretion must therefore be limited to examining whether it has been vitiated by manifest error or misuse of powers, or whether the institution concerned has manifestly exceeded the limits of its discretion.

59 So far as concerns the first condition, it is sufficient that, as follows from paragraphs 36 to 39 of this judgment, the measures on the organization of working time which form the subject-matter of the directive, save for that contained in the second sentence of Article 5, contribute directly to the improvement of health and safety protection for workers within the meaning of Article 118a, and cannot therefore be regarded as unsuited to the purpose of achieving the objective pursued.

60 The second condition is also fulfilled. Contrary to the view taken by the applicant, the Council did not commit any manifest error in concluding that the contested measures were necessary to achieve the objective of protecting the health and safety of workers.

61 In the first place, Article 4, which concerns the mandatory rest break, applies only if the working day is longer than six hours. Moreover, the relevant details, particularly the duration of the break and the terms on which it is granted, are to be laid down in collective agreements or agreements between the two sides of industry or, failing that, by national legislation. Finally, that provision may be the subject of several derogations, relating either to the status of the worker (Article 17(1)) or to the nature or characteristics of the activity pursued (Article 17(2), points 2.1 and 2.2), to be implemented by means of collective agreements or agreements concluded between the two sides of industry at national or regional level (Article 17(3)).

62 Second, the minimum uninterrupted weekly rest period of twenty-four hours provided for by the first sentence of Article 5, plus the eleven hours' daily rest referred to in Article 3, may be the subject of the same derogations as those authorized in relation to Article 4, referred to above. Further derogations relate to shift work activities and activities involving periods of work split up over the day (Article 17(2), point 2.3). In addition, the reference period of seven days may be extended to fourteen days (Article 16(1)).

63 Third, as regards Article 6(2), which provides that the average working time for each seven-day period is not to exceed forty-eight hours, Member States may lay down

a reference period not exceeding four months (Article 16(2)), which may in certain cases be extended to six months for the application of Article 17(2), points 2.1 and 2.2, and 17(3) (Article 17(4), first sentence), or even to twelve months (Article 17(4), second sentence). Article 18(1)(b)(i) even authorizes Member States, under certain conditions, not to apply Article 6.

64 Fourth, in relation to Article 7 concerning paid annual leave of four weeks, Article 18(1)(b)(ii) authorizes Member States to allow a transitional period of three years, during which workers must be entitled to three weeks' paid annual leave.

65 Finally, as to the applicant's argument that adoption of the contested directive was unnecessary since Directive 89/391 already applies to the areas covered by the contested directive, it is sufficient to note that Directive 89/391, as stated in Article 1 thereof, merely lays down, in order to encourage improvements in the health and safety of workers at work, general principles, as well as general guidelines for their implementation, concerning the prevention of occupational risks, the protection of health and safety, the elimination of risk and accident factors, and the provision of information to, consultation, participation and training of workers and their representatives. It is not therefore apt to achieve the objective of harmonizing minimum rest periods, rest breaks and a maximum limit to weekly working time, which form the subject-matter of the contested directive.

66 It follows that, in taking the view that the objective of harmonizing national legislation on the health and safety of workers, while maintaining the improvements made, could not be achieved by measures less restrictive than those that are the subject-matter of the directive, the Council did not commit any manifest error.

67 In the light of all the foregoing considerations, the plea of breach of the principle of proportionality must also be rejected.

Reason

The plea of misuse of powers

68 According to the applicant, the directive encompasses a number of measures that have no objective connection with its purported aims, and must therefore be annulled in its entirety. Those measures overshadow the very small elements - minimum daily rest periods, restrictions on maximum duration of night work - where scientific evidence indicates that there may be some causal connection with health and safety. Those two elements, in respect of which limited and specific action might have been justifiable, have instead been addressed in an unspecific, generalized, and thus unlawful manner.

69 The Court' s case-law (see, in particular, Case C-156/93 Parliament v Commission [1995] ECR I-2019, paragraph 31) defines misuse of powers as the adoption by a Community institution of a measure with the exclusive or main purpose of achieving an end other than that stated or evading a procedure specifically prescribed by the Treaty for dealing with the circumstances of the case.

 Alert

70 As is apparent from the Court' s examination of the plea of defective legal base, the Council could properly found the directive on Article 118a of the Treaty. The applicant has failed to establish that the directive was adopted with the exclusive or main purpose of achieving an end other than the protection of the health and safety of workers.

71 In those circumstances, the plea of misuse of powers must be rejected.

Reason Four

The plea of infringement of essential procedural requirements

72 The applicant' s primary submission is that the directive is inadequately reasoned. It does not clearly and unequivocally disclose the reasoning of the Community authority which adopted it, because it fails to demonstrate the causal connection relied on by the Community legislature between health and safety, on the one hand, and most of the measures it contains concerning working time (Articles 3, 4, 5, 6(2), 7 and 8), on the other. Nor, moreover, does the preamble to the directive explain why Community action was necessary.

73 In the alternative, the applicant submits that the directive is defectively reasoned, in that the legislature should have explained that many of its elements were concerned with the improvement of the living and working conditions of employees or with the social dimension of the internal market, rather than referring, as it did, to the health and safety of workers.

74 As to those arguments, whilst the reasoning required by Article 190 of the EC Treaty must show clearly and unequivocally the reasoning of the Community authority which adopted the contested measure so as to enable the persons concerned to ascertain the reasons for it and to enable the Court to exercise judicial review, the authority is not required to go into every relevant point of fact and law (see Case C-122/94 *Commission v Council* [1996] ECR I-881, paragraph 29).

75 In the case of the directive, the preamble clearly shows that the measures introduced are intended to harmonize the protection of the health and safety of workers.

76 Thus, the first, third, fourth and ninth recitals in the preamble refer respectively to Article 118a of the Treaty, to Directive 89/391 on the introduction of measures to encourage improvements in the safety and health of workers at work, to the Community Charter of the Fundamental Social Rights of Workers, and to the principles of the International Labour Organization with regard to the organization of working time.

77 So, too the fifth, seventh, eighth and eleventh to fifteenth recitals point to a direct link between the various measures on the organization of work laid down by the directive and the protection of the health and safety of workers.

78 The argument that the Council should have included in the preamble to the directive specific references to scientific material justifying the adoption of the various measures which it contains must be rejected.

79 As stated in paragraph 39 of this judgment, Article 118a does not require scientific proof to be produced for every measure adopted on the basis of that provision. Moreover, the Court has held that, where a contested measure clearly discloses the essential objective pursued by the institution, it would be pointless to require a specific statement of reasons for each of the technical choices made by it (see Case C-122/94 *Commission v Council*, cited above, paragraph 29).

80 Nor can the argument to the effect that the preamble to the directive fails to explain the need for Community action be accepted as well founded.

81 As has been pointed out in paragraphs 75 to 77 of this judgment, the preamble to the directive shows that the Council considered it necessary, in order to ensure an improved level of health and safety protection of workers, to take action to harmonize the national legislation of the Member States on the organization of working time. As stated in paragraph 47, the pursuit of such an objective, laid down in Article 118a itself, through harmonization by means of minimum requirements, necessarily presupposes Community-wide action.

82 Finally, as regards the arguments concerning alleged errors of assessment in the preamble to the directive, it is sufficient to refer to the Court's case-law to the effect that such questions relate not to the issue of infringement of essential procedural requirements but to the substance of the case (see, in particular, Joined Cases C-296/93 and C-307/93 *France and Ireland v Commission* [1996] ECR I-795, paragraph 76), and to recall that those questions have been examined in the context of the plea of defective legal base.

83 It follows that the plea of infringement of essential procedural requirements must also be rejected.

84 The application must accordingly be dismissed, save as regards the second sentence of Article 5 of the directive, which is to be annulled.

2 Administrative Law: Internal Enforcement

2.1 Preliminary Reference Procedure: Article 267 (ex 234) EC

***Fiorini Cristini (nee Cristini) v Société Nationale des Chemins de fer Français,* Case 32/75 [1976] 1 CMLR 573**

Panel: R. Lecourt P; J. Mertens de Wilmars, Lord Mackenzie Stuart, A. M. Donner, R. Monaco, P. Pescatore, H. Kutscher, M. Sørensen and A. O'Keeffe JJ. Sig. Alberto Trabucchi, Advocate General

Legislation: Regulation 1612/68

Facts: The *Cristini* case is an example of how the preliminary reference procedure can be such a complete referral that it borders on an actual substantive judgment. The case concerns on freedom of movement for workers and social and tax advantages.

> JUDGMENT
>
> 1 by judgment of 14 March 1975 which reached the court on 21 March, the Cour d'Appel, Paris, called upon the court, pursuant to Article 177 of the EEC Treaty, to give a ruling on the issue whether the reduction card issued by the Societe Nationale des Chemins de fer Francais for large families constitutes, for the workers of the Member States, a 'social advantage' within the meaning of Article 7 of Regulation (EEC) no 1612/68 of the Council of the European Communities of 15 October 1968 on freedom of movement for workers within the Community (oj l 257 of 19 October 1968).
>
> 2 It emerges from the judgment making the reference that the main action is concerned with the refusal by the SNCF of the request for such a reduction card, submitted by an Italian national, residing in France, whose husband, also of Italian nationality, worked in France where he died as the result of an industrial accident, leaving his widow and four infant children.
>
> 3 The refusal of the request, on the ground of the appellant's nationality, was based on provisions of French law which state that the reduction card for large families is in principle reserved solely for French nationals and that it is only issued to foreigners whose country of origin has entered into a reciprocal Treaty with France on this particular subject, which is not the case so far as Italy is concerned.
>
> 4 The French law of 29 October 1921, as amended by the law of 24 December 1940 and the decree of 3 November 1961, provides that in families of three or more children under the age of eighteen years the father, the mother and each child shall, at the request of the head of the family, receive an identity card entitling them to certain reductions in the fares of the SNCF.

5 Article 20 of the code Francais de la Famille et de l'aide Sociale (French Family and Social Security Code) (decree of 24 January 1956) provides that for the purpose of assisting families in bringing up their children, they shall be granted certain allowances and benefits, which are listed, albeit not exhaustively, and include, apart from family benefits provided for by the social security legislation and tax reductions or exemptions, reductions in the railway fares prescribed by the law concerned in the present case.

6 Although the court, when giving a ruling under Article 177, has no jurisdiction to apply the Community rule to a specific case, or, consequently, to pronounce upon a provision of national law, it may however provide the national court with the factors of interpretation depending on Community law which might be useful to it in evaluating the effects of such provision.

7 Article 7 (1) of Regulation (EEC) no 1612/68 of the Council of 15 October 1968 provides that a worker who is a national of a Member State may not, in the territory of the other Member States, be treated differently from national workers by reason of his nationality in respect of any conditions of employment and work.

8 Under paragraph (2) of that Article he is to enjoy 'the same social and tax advantages as national workers '.

9 Under paragraph (3) of that Article he must also, 'by virtue of the same right and under the same conditions as national workers, have access to training in vocational schools and retaining centres '.

10 The respondent in the main action has argued that the advantages thus prescribed are exclusively those attaching to the status of worker since they are connected with the contract of employment itself.

11 Although it is true that certain provisions in this Article refer to relationships deriving from the contract of employment, there are others, such as those concerning reinstatement and re-employment should a worker become unemployed, which have nothing to do with such relationships and even imply the termination of a previous employment.

12 In these circumstances the reference to 'social advantages' in Article 7 (2) cannot be interpreted restrictively.

13 It therefore follows that, in view of the equality of treatment which the provision seeks to achieve, the substantive area of application must be delineated so as to include all social and tax advantages, whether or not attached to the contract of employment, such as reductions in fares for large families.

14 It then becomes necessary to examine whether such an advantage must be granted to the widow and children after the death of the migrant worker when the national law provides that, at the request of the head of the family, each member of the family shall be issued with an identity card entitling him or her to the reduction.

15 If the widow and infant children of a national of the Member State in question are entitled to such cards provided that the request had been made by the father before his

death, the same must apply where the deceased father was a migrant worker and a national of another Member State.

16 It would be contrary to the purpose and the spirit of the Community rules on freedom of movement for workers to deprive the survivors of such a benefit following the death of the worker whilst granting the same benefit to the survivors of a national.

17 In this respect it is important to note the provisions of Regulation (EEC) no 1251/70 of the Commission on the right of workers to remain in the territory of a Member State after having been employed in that state.

18 Article 3 (1) of that Regulation provides that if a worker has acquired the right to remain in the territory of a Member State, the members of his family who are residing with him shall be entitled to remain there after his death, whilst Article 7 provides that: 'the right to equality of treatment, established by Council Regulation (EEC) no 1612/68, shall apply also to persons coming under the provisions of this Regulation '.

19 Accordingly the answer to the question should be that Article 7 (2) of Regulation (EEC) no 1612/68 of the Council must be interpreted as meaning that the social advantages referred to by that provision include fares reduction cards issued by a national railway authority to large families and that this applies, even if the said advantage is only sought after the worker's death, to the benefit of his family remaining in the same Member State.

3   Administrative Law: External Enforcement

3.1 Defences to Public Enforcement Actions Against National Governments Articles 258 (ex Art 226) and 259 (ex Art 227)

Commission of the European Communities v Belgium Case 42/89 [1992] 1 CMLR 22

Panel: Due CJ, Schockweiler and Zuleeg PPC; Mancini, Joliet, O'Higgins, Moitinho de Almeida, Rodríguez Iglesias and Grévisse JJ. Herr Carl Otto Lenz, Advocate-General

Legislation: Art 258 (ex Art 226, ex Art 169)

Facts: In arguing that the complexity of construction works at a water station in a Belgian town meant that the authorities needed a longer time to comply with the European norm, the Belgian government pleaded administrative difficulties and economic problems. This argument was not accepted on the facts.

JUDGMENT

1 By an application lodged at the Court Registry on 20 February 1989, the Commission of the European Communities brought an action under Article 169 of the EEC Treaty for a declaration that by not adopting within the prescribed period the laws, regulations and administrative provisions necessary to comply with the provisions of Council Directive 80/778/EEC of 15 July 1980 relating to the quality of water intended for human consumption (Official Journal 1980 L 229, p. 11), and in particular Articles 1, 2, 9, 18, 19 and 20 thereof, the Kingdom of Belgium has failed to fulfil its obligations under the EEC Treaty.

2 The action in this case has its origin in the finding by the Commission, in the first place, that the Royal Decree of 27 April 1984 transposing the directive into Belgian law (Moniteur Belge 1984, p. 9860) is not in conformity with Article 9(1)(b) and (3) of that directive inasmuch as it allows derogations from the provisions of the directive under conditions which are less stringent than those prescribed by the directive (Article 5 of the Royal Decree) and excludes from its scope water drawn by private individuals for household use (Article 1 of the Royal Decree), and, secondly, that the water supplied to the town of Verviers does not, in view of its lead content, comply with the requirements set out in the directive.

3 On 4 August 1986, the Commission, pursuant to the first paragraph of Article 169 of the Treaty, issued a formal notice to the Belgian Government mentioning the infringement of the provisions of the directive prohibiting certain derogations and the infringement relating to the inadequate quality of the water in Verviers. On 15 December 1987 the Commission issued a further notice to the Belgian Government concerning the exclusion from the measures transposing the directive of water drawn by private individuals for household use. Since it considered that the Belgian Government's reply was not such as to cause it to withdraw those objections, the Commission on 16 May 1988 issued a reasoned opinion giving the Belgian Government a period of two months within which to take the measures necessary to comply therewith. ...

The court set out the mechanics of the complaint and then set out the Belgian's governments responses, below.

22 The Belgian Government contended before the Court that owing to the cost and complexity of the construction works at the water treatment station which were needed in order that the town of Verviers might be supplied with water in conformity with the requirements of the directive, it will be possible to comply with those requirements only towards the end of 1990. That situation underlies the request made by the Belgian Government on 17 January 1989 under Article 20 of the directive for a longer period for complying with Annex 1 to the directive.

23 It should be observed in that connection that a request for a longer period for complying with Annex 1 must, in accordance with Article 20 of the directive, be made within the period laid down in Article 19 for the transposition of the directive into national law. After the expiry of that period derogations are permissible only in the

case of serious accidents and under the conditions laid down in Article 10 of the directive. The request by the Belgian Government was made more than four years after expiry of the abovementioned period.

24 As regards, finally, the difficulties, pleaded by the Belgian Government, in ensuring that the water supplied to the town of Verviers is in conformity with the directive, it should be borne in mind that, according to the case-law of the Court, a Member State may not plead practical or administrative difficulties in order to justify non-compliance with the obligations and time-limits laid down in Community directives. The same holds true of financial difficulties, which it is for the Member States to overcome by adopting appropriate measures.

 Alert

25 It follows that the Commission's claim that the Verviers drinking-water supply is not in conformity with the requirements set out in the directive is well founded.

26 It must therefore be held that by permitting the Walloon Region to allow the maximum admissible concentrations set out in Annex 1 to Council Directive 80/778 of 15 July 1980 relating to the quality of water intended for human consumption to be exceeded in circumstances other than those provided for in that directive, and the supply to Verviers of drinking water not in conformity with the requirements laid down in the same directive, the Kingdom of Belgium has failed to fulfil its obligations under the Treaty.

3.2 Standing to Contest Legality of Community Acts: Art 263 (ex Art 230)

Applicants for standing can be privileged or non-privileged. The latter category face a far tougher challenge in bringing an Article 263 (ex 230) action and are covered by Art 267. It provides that procedures can be instituted by any natural or legal person against a decision addressed to that person, or against a decision which, although in a form of regulation or a decision addressed to another person, is of direct and individual concern to the former.

If the decision is not directly addressed to the person bringing the action, they must show that they are a *de facto addressee* – the decision is of *direct and individual concern* to the applicant. In the next case, the Court came up with the so-called 'closed category test'.

Plaumann and Co. v Commission of the European Economic Community Case 25/62 [1964] CMLR 29

Panel: A. M. Donner P; L. Delvaux, R. Lecourt, Ch. L. Hammes, R. Rossi, A. Trabucchi and W. Strauss JJ. Herr Karl Roemer, Advocate-General

Legislation: Art 259 (ex Art 227, ex Art 173)

Facts: Plaumann, a trader in clementines, sought to challenge the Commission's decision regarding the collection of duties on importation of clementines from non-EU countries. The question was whether or not Plaumann fell into a 'closed category'.

JUDGMENT

I - on the application for annulment

Admissibility

Under the second paragraph of Article 173 of the EEC Treaty 'any natural or legal person may...institute proceedings against a Decision...which, although in the form of...a Decision addressed to another person, is of direct and individual concern to the former '. The defendant contends that the words 'other person' in this paragraph do not refer to Member States in their capacity as sovereign authorities and that individuals may not therefore bring an action for annulment against the Decisions of the Commission or of the Council addressed to Member States.

However the second paragraph of Article 173 does allow an individual to bring an action against Decisions addressed to 'another person' which are of direct and individual concern to the former, but this Article neither defines nor limits the scope of these words. The words and the natural meaning of this provision justify the broadest interpretation. Moreover provisions of the Treaty regarding the right of interested parties to bring an action must not be interpreted restrictively. Therefore, the Treaty being silent on the point, a limitation in this respect may not be presumed.

It follows that the defendant's argument cannot be regarded as well founded.

The defendant further contends that the contested Decision is by its very nature a Regulation in the form of an individual Decision and therefore action against it is no more available to individuals than in the case of legislative measures of general application.

It follows however from Articles 189 and 191 of the EEC Treaty that Decisions are characterized by the limited number of persons to whom they are addressed. In order to determine whether or not a measure constitutes a Decision one must enquire whether that measure concerns specific persons. The contested Decision was addressed to the government of the Federal Republic of Germany and refuses to grant it authorization for the partial suspension of customs duties on certain products imported from third countries. Therefore the contested measure must be regarded as a Decision referring to a particular person and binding that person alone.

Under the second paragraph of Article 173 of the Treaty private individuals may institute proceedings for annulment against Decisions which, although addressed to another person, are of direct and individual concern to them, but in the present case the defendant denies that the contested Decision is of direct and individual concern to the applicant.

It is appropriate in the first place to examine whether the second requirement of admissibility is fulfilled because, if the applicant is not individually concerned by the Decision, it becomes unnecessary to enquire whether he is directly concerned.

Persons other than those to whom a Decision is addressed may only claim to be individually concerned if that Decision affects them by reason of certain attributes which are peculiar to them or by reason of circumstances in which they are differentiated from all other persons and by virtue of these factors distinguishes them individually just as in the case of the person addressed. In the present case the applicant is affected by the disputed Decision as an importer of clementines, that is to say, by reason of a commercial activity which may at any time be practised by any person and is not therefore such as to distinguish the applicant in relation to the contested Decision as in the case of the addressee. ...

Plea for Illegality and Grounds For Review: Art 277 (ex Art 241)

3.3 Infringement of the Treaty or any Rule Relating to its Application – Proportionality

Many of the cases under this heading are Common Agricultural Policy cases, because the very nature of the scheme is such that it involves value judgments about identifiable policy objectives (usually to do with the disposal of some 'lake' or 'mountain' of food stuffs that no-one in Europe wants to consume, but farmers like to produce).

Bela-Mühle Josef Bergmann KG v Grows-Farm GmbH & CO, Case 114/76 [1979] 2 CMLR 83

Panel: Kutscher CJ; Donner and Pescatore PPC; Mertens de Wilmars, Sørensen, Lord Mackenzie Stuart, O'Keeffe, Bosco and Touffait JJ. Sig. Francesco Capotorti, Advocate-General

Legislation: Art 277 (ex Art 241, ex Art 177)

Facts: Farmers were required to buy animal feeding stuffs containing skimmed milk, (which had displaced the cheaper soya), as a method of dealing with the EU milk lake. They argued that this was disproportionate, in that it enforced an excessive burden onto individual farmers to try and address a broad, policy objective.

JUDGMENT

1 by order of 8 September 1976, which reached the court on 2 December 1976, the Landgericht Oldenburg asked the court under Article 177 of the EEC Treaty for a ruling on the validity of Council Regulation (EEC) no 563/76 of 15 March 1976 on the compulsory purchase of skimmed-milk powder held by intervention agencies for use in feeding-stuffs (OJ l 67, p. 18). The reference was made in connexion with civil proceedings concerning the performance of a contract for delivery of feeding-stuffs concluded between a producer of concentrated feeding-stuffs, the plaintiff in the main action, and the proprietor of a battery hen unit, the defendant in the main action. In addition to the price agreed under the contract the plaintiff in the main action asked for payment of a sum equivalent to the charge arising under Regulation (EEC) no 563/76 the validity of which is, however, contested by the defendant in the main action.

2 Regulation (EEC) no 563/76 was promulgated at a time when the stocks of skimmed-milk powder bought in by the intervention agencies pursuant to Regulation (EEC) no 804/68 of the Council of 27 June 1968 on the common organization of the market in milk and milk products (OJ English special edition 1968, p. 176) had reached

considerable proportions and were continuing to increase despite the measures adopted by the Community institutions to curb the tendency towards over-production of milk and to increase the sale of skimmed-milk powder. The system established by Regulation (EEC) no 563/76 the application of which was not extended beyond the end of the original period of application, which expired on 31 October 1976, was designed to reduce stocks through the increased use in feeding-stuffs of the protein contained in skimmed-milk powder. To this end the Regulation made the grant of the aids provided for certain vegetable protein products as well as the free circulation in the Community of certain imported animal feed products subject to the obligation to purchase specified quantities of skimmed-milk powder. In order to ensure that this obligation was fulfilled the grant of aid and free circulation were subject to the provision of a security or the production, on the prescribed form, of evidence of the purchase and of the denaturing of the prescribed quantities of skimmed-milk powder.

3 Under Article 1 of Commission Regulation (EEC) no 753/76 of 31 March 1976 laying down detailed rules for the sale of skimmed-milk powder for use in animal feed (OJ l 88, p. 1), skimmed-milk powder held by the intervention agencies was resold by them in fulfilment of the obligation to purchase at a price of 52.16 U.A. Per 100 kg multiplied by a coefficient which, in the case of the Federal Republic of Germany, amounted to 0.8325. The denaturing costs to be borne by the purchaser were between 1 and 3 U.A. Per 100 kg. During the period when Regulation (EEC) no 563/76 applied, the market price of soya oil cake, a vegetable product with a nutritional value comparable to that of skimmed-milk powder for use in animal feed other than that for young calves, varied between 13.30 and 20.40 U.A. Per 100 kg, the average being about 18 U.A. Per 100 kg. The compulsory purchase of skimmed-milk powder was, therefore, imposed at a price equal to about three times its value as animal feed. The security, which was released only on production of proof of the purchase of a specified quantity of powdered skimmed milk, was fixed at such an amount that, if it was forfeited, its effect on the prices of feeding-stuffs was slightly more than the increase due to the purchase of powdered skimmed milk.

4 Article 5 of the Regulation laid down that, in the case of contracts concluded before the date of entry into force of the Regulation, the burden of the costs arising under the arrangements was to be borne by the successive buyers of the products in question. The Regulation did not contain any similar provision making it possible for consumers of feeding-stuffs, such as breeders of poultry and pigs, to incorporate the increase in the price of their products.

5 The validity of these arrangements has been contested on grounds of conflict in particular with the objectives of the common agricultural policy as defined in Article 39 of the Treaty, the prohibition of discrimination laid down in the second subparagraph of Article 40 (3) and the principle of proportionality between the means employed and the end in view. Because of the close connexion between these grounds of complaint, it will be appropriate to consider them together.

6 Under Article 39, the objectives of the common agricultural policy are to be the rational development of agricultural production, the assurance of a fair standard of living for the whole of the agricultural Community, the stabilization of markets and the

availability of supplies to consumers at reasonable prices. Although Article 39 thus enables the common agricultural policy to be defined in terms of a wide choice of measures involving guidance or intervention, the fact nevertheless remains that the second subparagraph of Article 40 (3) provides that the common organization of the agricultural markets shall be limited to pursuit of the objectives set out in Article 39. Furthermore, the same subparagraph lays down that the common organization of the markets ' shall exclude any discrimination between producers or consumers within the Community'. Thus the statement of the objectives contained in Article 39, taken together with the rules in the second subparagraph of Article 40 (3), supplies both positive and negative criteria by which the legality of the measures adopted in this matter may be appraised.

7 The arrangements made by Regulation (EEC) no 563/76 constituted a temporary measure intended to counteract the consequences of a chronic imbalance in the common organization of the market in milk and milk products. A feature of these arrangements was the imposition not only on producers of milk and milk products but also, and more especially, on producers in other agricultural sectors of a financial burden which took the form, first, of the compulsory purchase of certain quantities of an animal feed product and, secondly, of the fixing of a purchase price for that product at a level three times higher than that of the substances which it replaced. The obligation to purchase at such a disproportionate price constituted a discriminatory distribution of the burden of costs between the various agricultural sectors. Nor, moreover, was such an obligation necessary in order to attain the objective in view, namely, the disposal of stocks of skimmed-milk powder. It could not therefore be justified for the purposes of attaining the objectives of the common agricultural policy.

8 In consequence, the answer must be that Council Regulation (EEC) no 563/76 of 15 March 1976 is null and void.

Further Reading

Arnull, Anthony; 'The Law Lords and the European Union: swimming with the incoming tide', [2010] ELR 57

Gari, Gabriel; Tridimas, Takis; 'Winners and losers in Luxembourg: a statistical analysis of judicial review before the European Court of Justice and the Court of First Instance (2001-2005)'; [2010] ELR 131

Direct Effect, Indirect Effect and State Liability

Topic List

Daryll Bewick

Introduction

The finding of individual remedies under an international treaty originally conceived as commercial and enforceable by States or EU institutions required a change of thinking on the part of the European Court of Justice (ECJ). This involved a move from the international law norm to one based upon the concept that as this is a 'new legal order' it needed new legal remedies. Such thinking inevitably engaged with fundamental and emotive issues such as state sovereignty. It was not usual for an international court to specify the way a state should absorb international rules and the need for case law was inevitable. This departure from the traditional international law approach allowed individuals to challenge both EU law and its implementation by the Member States in a way not possible without it. As a result any EU measures, not just those that were directly applicable (and so part of the national law) were opened up to challenge.

1 Direct and Indirect Effect

It is perhaps difficult to perceive the radical nature of the decision in the 1963 case of *NV Algemene Transporten Expeditie Onderneming van Gend en Loos v Nederlandse Administratie der Berlingen* Case 26/62 [1963] CMLR 105 after it has been around for so many years. During those years its basic message has been added to and pushed and pulled in different directions. It perhaps just seems as if it ought to be have been there from the start. Radical though it may have been, *van Gend en Loos* has quickly spawned a small family of remedies designed to address the issue of individual losses resulting from the interplay of State and EU legislation. This family is the subject of the present chapter and, dysfunctional though it undoubtedly is, serves to illustrate some imaginative attempts to grapple with the legal problems presented by a developing Community.

NV Algemene Transporten Expeditie Onderneming van Gend en Loos v Nederlandse Administratie der Berlingen **Case 26/62 [1963] CMLR 105**

Panel: Donner P, Delvaux, Rossi, Riese, Hammes, Trabucchi and Lecourt, JJ. Herr Karl Roemer, Advocate-General

Legislation: Art 30 (ex Art 25, ex Art 12)

Facts: In 1960 van Gend en Loos (a Dutch company) imported a quantity of the chemical emulsion ureaformaldehyde from Germany into the Netherlands. Due to a recent change in the classification of this substance the Dutch tariff charged upon its import had risen from 3% to 8%. As a result van Gend en Loos appealed to the national Dutch Inspector of Import and Excise Duties and then to an internal tribunal (the Nederlandse Tariefcommissie) that the imposition of this increase after the entry into force of the EEC Treaty violated Art 30 (ex Art 25) of the Treaty. The Tariefcommissie duly referred two questions to the ECJ:

(a)   Whether Art 30 could be applied within a Member State by the citizens of that Member State enforcing individual rights which could be protected by the national courts.

(b)   If this were so whether the increase of the duty to 8% was an illegal increase within the meaning of Art 30 or simply a reasonable alteration that was not so prohibited.

ADVOCATE-GENERAL ROEMER

He who is familiar with the law of the Community knows that in fact it is not restricted to the contractual relations between a number of States viewed as subjects of the law of nations. The Community has its own institutions, independent of the member-States, endowed with the power to take administrative action and to issue legal rules which directly create rights and obligations not only for the member-States and their administrative authorities but also for the nationals of the member-States. We can deduce this clearly from Articles 187, 189, 191 and 192 of the Treaty.

Nonetheless as far as the broad issues concerning import and export duties were concerned:

The subtle terminology of the Treaty, the material contents and the context surely imply … only an obligation on the member-States.

Further, we find a whole series of provisions which according to their content and context, although drafted in the form of a declaration, clearly envisage only obligations of the member-States and not direct internal legal effects… .

He went on to advise that internal effect was not possible here:

…large parts of the Treaty certainly contain obligations on the member-States only, and do not contain rules with a direct internal effect.

Despite this opinion the ECJ found the opposite, declaring a result in favour of van Gend en Loos and against the Dutch government. It expressed its reasons for such a judgement in the following terms:

JUDGMENT

The first question posed by the Tariefcommissie is whether Article 12 of the Treaty has an immediate effect in internal law, in that nationals of the member-States could, on the basis of the Article, enforce rights which the national court should protect.

To know whether the provisions of an international treaty have such an effect it is necessary to look at its spirit, its economic aspect and the terms used.

The purpose of the E.E.C. Treaty—to create a Common Market, the functioning of which directly affects the citizens of the Community—implies that this Treaty is more than an agreement creating only mutual obligations between the contracting parties. This interpretation is confirmed by the preamble to the Treaty which, in addition to mentioning governments, affects individuals. The creation of organs institutionalising

Decipher
The first two terms are perhaps a little unusual for an English lawyer more familiar with the literal approach.

certain sovereign rights, the exercise of which affects both member-States and citizens is a particular example. In addition, the nationals of the States, united into the Community, are required to collaborate in the functioning of that Community, by means of the European Parliament and the Economic and Social Council. Furthermore, the role of the Court of Justice in the framework of Article 177, the aim of which is to ensure uniformity of interpretation of the Treaty by the national courts, confirms that the States recognised in Community law have an authority capable of being invoked by their nationals before those courts. We must conclude from this that the Community constitutes a new legal order in international law, for whose benefit the States have limited their sovereign rights, albeit within limited fields, and the subjects of which comprise not only the member-States but also their nationals. Community law, therefore, apart from legislation by the member-States, not only imposes obligations on individuals but also confers on them legal rights. The latter arise not only when an explicit grant is made by the Treaty, but also through obligations imposed, in a clearly defined manner, by the Treaty on individuals as well as on member-States and the Community institutions. ...

Alert

The text of Article 12 sets out a clear and unconditional prohibition, which is not a duty to act but a duty not to act. This duty is imposed without any power in the States to subordinate its application to a positive act of internal law. The prohibition is perfectly suited by its nature to produce direct effects in the legal relations between the member-States and their citizens.

The carrying out of Article 12 does not require legislative intervention by the States. The fact that the Article designates the member-States as subject to the duty to abstain does not imply that their nationals may not be the beneficiaries of the duty.

The fact that the Treaty, in the aforementioned Articles, allows the Commission and the member-States to bring before the Court a State which has not carried out its obligations, does not imply that individuals may not invoke these obligations, in appropriate cases, before a national court; and likewise, the fact that the Treaty puts at the disposal of the Commission means to ensure respect for the duties imposed on those subject to it does not exclude the possibility of invoking violation of these obligations in litigation between individuals before national courts. To limit the sanctions against violation of Article 12 by member-States merely to the procedures laid down in Articles 169 and 170 would remove all direct judicial protection of the individual rights of their nationals. Reliance on these Articles would risk being ineffective if it had to be exercised after the enforcement of a national decision which misinterpreted the requirements of the Treaty. The vigilance of individuals interested in protecting their rights creates an effective control additional to that entrusted by Articles 169 and 170 to the diligence of the Commission and the member-States.

For these reasons, according to the spirit, the economic aspect and the terms of the Treaty, Article 12 should be interpreted in such a sense as to produce direct effect and to create individual rights which internal courts should protect.

Links

1. Note 'clear and unconditional' legislation is now what is looked for to establish direct effect.
2. By emphasising the negative duty the court created subsequent doubt whether direct effect could apply to a positive duty.

Decipher

Note the ECJ's interchange between direct application and direct effect at this early stage.

> Article 12 of the E.E.C. Treaty has direct application within the territory of a member-State and enures the benefit of citizens whose individual rights the internal courts should protect. ...

van Gend en Loos is the case that starts the whole direct effect ball rolling. Notice how the European Court of Justice does not follow the advice of the Advocate-General, who despite beginning with a recognition that individual rights could exist under the Treaty ultimately pulls back from this conclusion with regard to Art 30. The Court not only decides that direct effect can apply to the Treaty generally but that it applies to Art 30 particularly.

As seen in this case a major area of weakness of the Treaty of Rome (as originally drafted) was that it failed to provide adequate measures of enforcement against those Member States who infringed Treaty obligations.

Article 226 (originally Article 169), for instance, while allowing the Commission to take an infringing State to the ECJ failed to specify a penalty of value to the individual EU citizen, nor a method by which such an individual could personally seek redress against such a State in their own national courts. This case tackled the issue head on, widening the scope by which the Treaty could be enforced by allowing the individual the right to enforce such obligations.

Having created direct effect the ECJ then logically had to go on to establish the supremacy of EU law over conflicting national law in cases such as *Costa v ENEL* Case 6/64 [1964] CMLR 425 and *Amministrazione delle Finanze Stato v Simmenthal SpA* Case 106/77 [1978] 3 CMLR 263.

It also had to consider whether the direct effect of Articles could be applied to actions between individuals (horizontal direct effect) in *Defrenne v SABENA (No 2)* Case 43/75 [1976] 2 CMLR 98.

Van Duyn v Home Office Case 41/74 [1975] 1 CMLR 1

Panel: Lecourt P, Ó Dálaigh, Lord Mackenzie Stuart, Donner, Monaco, Mertens de Wilmars, Pescatore, Kutscher and Sørensen, JJ. M. Henri Mayras, Advocate-General

Legislation: Art 45 (ex Art 39); Directive 64/221

Facts: The UK government considered the Church of Scientology of California to be a 'pseudo-philosophical cult' that was socially harmful albeit not unlawful. In an attempt to curb its growth foreign Scientologists were prevented from entering the country to study or work.

Yvonne Van Duyn, a Dutch national, landed at Gatwick airport to take up a secretary's job at the Church's headquarters in East Grinstead, Surrey, only to be sent back to the Netherlands by UK immigration the same day. As a consequence she began a High Court action invoking Article 45 and Directive 64/221 to allege a breach of her right of freedom of movement.

The High Court asked three preliminary questions of the ECJ:

1   Was Article 45 directly effective?

2   Was Directive 64/221 directly effective?

3   Could membership of a cult be considered 'personal conduct' entitling the UK to refuse entry for reasons of public policy?

It is question two (could a directive be given direct effect) that is the area of interest here but the examination of question one also served to reinforce the developed principles.

ADVOCATE-GENERAL HENRI MAYRAS

'The first question will not delay us.

The criteria which have over several years emerged from your case law to determine whether a provision of Community law, and in particular a rule laid down in the EEC Treaty, is directly applicable in the sense that it confers on individuals rights on which they can rely in proceedings before national courts, are clearly fixed:

- the provision must impose on the member-States a clear and precise obligation;

- it must be unconditional, *i.e.*, not accompanied by any reservation; if, however, it is subject to certain exceptions, they must be strictly defined and delimited;

- finally, the application of the Community rule must not be conditional on any subsequent legislation either of the Community institutions or of those of the member-States, and must not lead to the latter having an effective power of discretionary judgment as to the application of the rule in question.'

He goes on to provide justifications for advancing the principle to directives in addition to articles and regulations:

'Less obvious is the solution to the second question which concerns, as we have seen, the direct applicability of the Council directive of 25 February 1964.

Article 189 of the Treaty distinguishes between regulations, which are not only binding but also directly applicable in the member-States, and directives, which are also binding, to be sure, for the States but which do not in principle have direct effect in so far as they leave to the States the choice of the methods of bringing them into operation.

But, keeping outside formal legal categories, you have held in *Grad v. Finanzamt Traunstein* (9/70), *Transports Lesage et Cie v. Hauptzollamt Freiburg* (20/70) and *Haselhorst v. Finanzamt Düsseldorf-Altstadt* (23/70) that, apart from regulations, other Community acts mentioned in Article 189 can produce direct effect, particularly in those cases in which the Community authorities have obliged the member-States to adopt a given behaviour; the effective power of such acts, you said, would be weakened if individuals could not, in such circumstances, rely in legal proceedings on the rights which are conferred on them by decisions of such nature, even though they were not enacted in the form of regulations.

 Decipher
Again note the interchangeability of the terms direct effect and direct applicability in these cases.

Even clearer is the statement in your judgment in *S.A.C.E. v. Italian Ministry of Finance* (33/70): a Directive, the purpose of which was to impose on a member-State a final date for the performance of a Community obligation, not only affects the relations between the Commission and that State but also entails consequences which may be invoked ... by individuals whenever *by its nature* the provision establishing this obligation is directly applicable.

Faced with a directive we must therefore examine in each case whether the wording, the nature and the logic of the provisions in question are capable of producing direct effects between the addressee member-States and their citizens.'

The ECJ answered the first two questions in the following way:

JUDGMENT

First Question

[4] By the first question, the Court is asked to say whether Article 48 of the EEC Treaty is directly applicable so as to confer on individuals rights enforceable by them in the courts of a member-State.

[5] It is provided, in Article 48 (1) and (2), that freedom of movement for workers shall be secured by the end of the transitional period and that such freedom shall entail 'the abolition of any discrimination based on nationality between workers of member-States as regards employment, remuneration and other conditions of work and employment' .

[6] These provisions impose on member-States a precise obligation which does not require the adoption of any further measure on the part either of the Community institutions or of the member-States and which leaves them, in relation to its implementation, no discretionary power.

[7] Paragraph (3), which defines the rights implied by the principle of freedom of movement for workers, subjects them to limitations justified on grounds of public policy, public security or public health. The application of these limitations is, however, subject to judicial control, so that a member-State's rights to invoke the limitations does not prevent the provisions of Article 48, which enshrine the principle of freedom of movement for workers, from conferring on individuals rights which are enforceable by them and which the national courts must protect.

[8] The reply to the first question must therefore be in the affirmative.

Second Question

[9] The second question asks the Court to say whether Council Directive 64/221 of 25 February 1964 on the co-ordination of special measures concerning the movement and residence of foreign nationals which are justified on grounds of public policy, public security or public health is directly applicable so as to confer on individuals rights enforceable by them in the courts of a member-State.

[10] It emerges from the order making the reference that the only provision of the Directive which is relevant is that contained in Article 3 (1) which provides that

Decipher

In these paragraphs the ECJ confirms that Art 45 satisfies the *van Gend en Loos* criteria.

'measures taken on grounds of public policy or public security shall be based exclusively on the personal conduct of the individual concerned'.

[11] The United Kingdom observes that, since Article 189 of the Treaty distinguishes between the effects ascribed to regulations, directives and decisions, it must therefore be presumed that the Council, in issuing a directive rather than making a regulation, must have intended that the directive should have an effect other than that of a regulation and accordingly that the former should not be directly applicable.

[12] If, however, by virtue of the provisions of Article 189 regulations are directly applicable and, consequently, may by their very nature have direct effects, it does not follow from this that other categories of acts mentioned in that Article can never have similar effects. It would be incompatible with the binding effect attributed to a directive by Article 189 to exclude, in principle, the possibility that the obligation which it imposes may be invoked by those concerned. In particular, where the Community authorities have, by directive, imposed on member-States the obligation to pursue a particular course of conduct, the useful effect of such an act would be weakened if individuals were prevented from relying on it before their national courts and if the latter were prevented from taking it into consideration as an element of Community law. Article 177, which empowers national courts to refer to the Court questions concerning the validity and interpretation of all acts of the Community institutions, without distinction, implies furthermore that these acts may be invoked by individuals in the national courts. It is necessary to examine, in every case, whether the nature, general scheme and wording of the provision in question are capable of having direct effects on the relations between member-States and individuals.

[13] By providing that measures taken on grounds of public policy shall be based exclusively on the personal conduct of the individual concerned, Article 3 (1) of Directive 64/221 is intended to limit the discretionary power which national laws generally confer on the authorities responsible for the entry and expulsion of foreign nationals. First, the provision lays down an obligation which is not subject to any exception or condition and which, by its very nature, does not require the intervention of any act on the part either of the institutions of the Community or of member-States. Secondly, because member-States are thereby obliged, in implementing a clause which derogates from one of the fundamental principles of the Treaty in favour of individuals, not to take account of factors extraneous to personal conduct, legal certainty for the persons concerned requires that they should be able to rely on this obligation even though it has been laid down in a legislative act which has no automatic direct effect in its entirety.

[14] If the meaning and exact scope of the provision raise questions of interpretation, these questions can be resolved by the courts, taking into account also the procedure under Article 177 of the Treaty.

[15] Accordingly, in reply to the second question, Article 3 (1) of Council Directive 64/221 of 25 February 1964 confers on individuals rights which are enforceable by them in the courts of a member-State and which the national courts must protect.

Decipher

Here the ECJ answers the UK arguments and justifies the extension of direct effect to the directives.

With regard to the third question the ECJ went on to find that associations which a person makes were part of 'personal conduct' and as such fell under the discretionary power to refuse entry given to member states under 'public policy'. Van Duyn lost her appeal.

Direct effect had been extended in its application from Articles to Regulations in *Franz Grad v Finanzamt Traunstein* Case 9/70 [1971] CMLR 1. However for a while it had been believed that directives were incapable of receiving direct effect due to their conditional nature (conditional upon implementation by a member state). *Van Duyn* was the case in which the ECJ grasped the nettle of unconditionality and decided that a directive could be directly effective.

However, further case law was necessary to establish an answer to the question: could a private company or individual have a directive enforced against them?

Marshall v Southampton and South West Hampshire Area Health Authority (Teaching) Case 152/84 [1986] 1 CMLR 688

Panel: Lord Mackenzie Stuart CJ, Everling and Bahlmann PPC, Bosco, Koopmans, Due and O'Higgins JJ. Sir Gordon Slynn, Advocate-General

Legislation: Directive 76/207

Facts: Miss Marshall had been employed as a Senior Dietician by the Health Authority from 1974 until 1980 when she was dismissed solely because she had reached the Authorities compulsory retirement age (of 60 for women and 65 for men). While she had in fact been allowed to work until she had reached 62 she claimed the differing retirement ages to be contrary to the Sex Discrimination Directive 76/207 as a result of which she had suffered financially and in terms of the satisfaction she obtained from her job. Her case reached the Employment Appeals Tribunal before a number of questions were raised as preliminary references to the ECJ. For our purpose the central issue was the contention of both the Authority and the UK government that a directive which has not been implemented cannot be relied on by one private individual against another; and that where the State is acting as an employer, it should be treated in the same way as a private employer.

ADVOCATE-GENERAL SLYNN

I remain, despite the arguments in this case and in the case of *Roberts*, of the view expressed in my opinion in *Becker* that a directive not addressed to an individual cannot of itself impose obligations on him. It is, in cases like the present, addressed to member-States and not to the individual. The obligations imposed by such a directive are on the member-States. Such a directive does not have to be notified to the individual and it is only published in the Official Journal by way of information—in my view far too tenuous a link with the individual concerned to create a legal obligation.

Despite the general phrases to which I have referred, I read the Court's judgment as saying implicitly, as I said explicitly, that a directive comes into play *only* to enable rights to be claimed by individuals against the State in default. The State cannot rely on its own failure to confer those rights. The citizen may assert them against the State either as a sword or as a shield.

To give what is called 'horizontal effect' to directives would totally blur the distinction between regulations and directives which the Treaty establishes in Articles 189 and 91

This reasoning was to be accepted by the ECJ:

JUDGMENT

[43] The respondent and the United Kingdom propose ... that a directive may, in certain specific circumstances, have direct effect as against a member-State in so far as the latter may not rely on its failure to perform its obligations under the directive. However, they maintain that a directive can never impose obligations directly on individuals and that it can only have direct effect against a member-State *qua* public authority and not against a member-State *qua* employer. As an employer a State is no different from a private employer. It would not therefore be proper to put persons employed by the State in a better position than those who are employed by a private employer.

[48] With regard to the argument that a directive may not be relied upon against an individual, it must be emphasised that according to Article 189 of the EEC Treaty the binding nature of a directive, which constitutes the basis for the possibility of relying on the directive before a national court, exists only in relation to 'each member-State to which it is addressed'. It follows that a directive may not of itself impose obligations on an individual and that a provision of a directive may not be relied upon as such against such a person. It must therefore be examined whether, in this case, the respondent must be regarded as having acted as an individual.

Alert

[49] In that respect it must be pointed out that where a person involved in legal proceedings is able to rely on a directive as against the State he may do so regardless of the capacity in which the latter is acting, whether as employer or public authority. In either case it is necessary to prevent the State from taking advantage of its own failure to comply with Community law.

[50] It is for the national court to apply those considerations to the circumstances of each case; the Court of Appeal has, however, stated in the order for reference that the respondent, Southampton and South West Hampshire Area Health Authority (Teaching), is a public authority.

Decipher

A public authority is an emanation of the state.

[51] The argument submitted by the United Kingdom that the possibility of relying on provisions of the directive against the respondent *qua* organ of the State would give rise to an arbitrary and unfair distinction between the rights of State employees and those of private employees does not justify any other conclusion. Such a distinction may easily be avoided if the member-State concerned has correctly implemented the directive in national law.

This case resolved the issue left as a natural consequence of *van Gend en Loos*.

Pubblico Ministero v Tullio Ratti **Case 148/78 [1980] 1 CMLR 96**

Panel: Mertens de Wilmars P, Lord Mackenzie Stuart PPC, Pescatore, Sørensen, O'Keeffe, Bosco and Touffait JJ. Herr Gerhard Reischl, Advocate-General

Legislation: Directives 73/173 and 77/728

Facts: An Italian company Silvam (represented in all that occurred in this case by Mr Ratti) packaged its solvents in containers the labels of which complied with EU Directive 73/173 and its varnishes in containers the labels of which complied with Directive 77/728. Neither Directive had been implemented by the Italian state (although the government still had time to implement Directive 77/728). Italy still enforced its own more stringent earlier law in this area. Mr Ratti was duly prosecuted for breaching this Italian law. The national court referred a number of issues to the ECJ amongst which the following two are of relevance here:

(a)   Did Directive 73/173 have direct effect and so confer individual rights which ought to be protected by the Italian court?

(b)   Did Directive 77/728 protect a person acting upon a legitimate expectation in complying with the requirements of a directive before the expiry of the period within which the member state must comply with the directive?

JUDGMENT

The answer to question one was self evident as long as the *van Gend en Loos* criteria could be satisfied and the Court duly announced this:

[1] As far as solvents are concerned, that legislation ought, at the material time, to have been amended in order to comply with Directive 73/173 of 4 June 1973, the provisions of which member-States were supposed to incorporate into their internal legal orders by 8 December 1974 at the latest, an obligation which the Italian Government has not fulfilled. ...

[4] That amendment would have resulted in the repeal of the provision of the Italian Act which the accused is charged with contravening and would consequently have altered the conditions for applying the criminal sanctions contained in the law in question...

[21] Particularly in cases in which the Community authorities have, by means of directive, placed member-States under a duty to adopt a certain course of action, the effectiveness of such an act would be weakened if persons were prevented from relying on it in legal proceedings and national courts prevented from taking it into consideration as an element of Community law. [22] Consequently a member-State which has not adopted the implementing measures required by the directive in the prescribed periods may not rely, as against individuals, on its own failure to perform the obligations which the directive entails. [23] It follows that a national court requested by a person who has complied with the provisions of a directive not to apply a national provision incompatible with the directive not incorporated into the internal legal order of a defaulting member-State, must uphold that request if the obligation in question is unconditional and sufficiently precise. [24] Therefore the answer to the first question must be that after the expiration of the period fixed for the implementation of a

directive a member-State may not apply its internal law—even if it is provided with penal sanctions—which has not yet been adapted in compliance with the directive, to a person who has complied with the requirements of the directive.

Question two, however was not so clear:

[5] As regards the packaging and labelling of varnishes, Directive 77/728 of 7 November 1977 had, at the material time, been adopted by the Council, but by virtue of Article 12 thereof member-States have until 9 November 1979 to bring into force the laws, regulations and administrative provisions necessary to comply therewith.

As a result could Directive 77/728 be:

[39] ...[I]immediately and directly applicable with regard to the obligations imposed on member-States to refrain from action as from the date of notification of that directive in a case where a person, acting upon a legitimate expectation, has complied with the provisions of that directive before the expiry of the period within which the member-State must comply with the said directive.

[40] The objective of that directive is analogous to that of Directive 73/173 in that it lays down similar rules for preparations intended to be used as paints, varnishes, printing inks, adhesives and similar products, and containing dangerous substances.

[41] Article 12 of that directive provides that member-States must implement it within 24 months of its notification, which took place on 9 November 1977. [42] That period has not yet expired and the States to which the directive was addressed have until 9 November 1979 to incorporate the provisions of Directive 77/728 into their internal legal orders. [43] It follows that, for the reasons expounded in the grounds of the answer to the national court's first question, it is only at the end of the prescribed period and in the event of the member-State's default that the directive—and in particular Article 9 thereof—will be able to have the effects described in the answer to the first question. [44] Until that date is reached the member-States remain free in that field. [45] If one member-State has incorporated the provisions of a directive into its internal legal order before the end of the period prescribed therein, that fact cannot produce any effect with regard to the other member-States.

[46] In conclusion, since a directive by its nature imposes obligations only on member-States, it is not possible for an individual to plead the principle of 'legitimate expectation' before the expiry of the period prescribed for its implementation. [47] Therefore the answer to the fifth question must be that Directive 77/728 of the Council of the European Communities of 7 November 1977 ... cannot bring about with respect to any individual who has complied with the provisions of the said directive before the expiration of the adaptation period prescribed for the member-State any effect capable of being taken into consideration by national courts.

 Decipher
It was the fact that Germany had already incorporated the directive and Silvam exported to Germany that had prompted Silvam to the early use of the directive.

Directives are conditional upon implementation into national law by a Member State. So, by definition, they automatically fail to fulfil the *van Gend en Loos* requirement of unconditionality. How could a directive ever be given direct effect in that case?

The answer was implicit within *Van Duyn* – they became unconditional when they have passed their date for implementation. At that point the *van Gend en Loos* criteria were satisfied, at that point direct effect 'crystallised'. *Ratti* neatly highlights this point.

The ground rules for the direct effect of a directive were beginning to slot into place. But the question remained: for the application of direct effect, how far did the concept of the 'State' extend?

Foster and Others v British Gas Plc Case 188/89 [1990] 2 CMLR 833

Panel: Slynn PC, Kakouris, Schockweiler and Zuleeg PPC, Mancini, Joliet, O'Higgins, Mohitinho de Almeida, Rodriguez Iglesias, Grévisse and Díez de Velasco JJ. Walter Van Gerven, Advocate-General

Legislation: Directive 76/207 Art 5(1)

Facts: Mrs Foster and other appellants were taking a sex discrimination action under Directive 76/207 against their compulsory retirement at 60 instead of the 65 required for male employees of the British Gas Corporation. The House of Lords submitted to the ECJ the sole question whether the BGC was a state body against which a directive could be applied.

ADVOCATE-GENERAL VAN GERVAN

'...in *Marshall* the Court stated that persons may only rely on provisions such as Article 5(1) of Directive 76/207 in their relations with 'the State,' in its capacity as 'employer or public authority,' since 'it is necessary to prevent the State from taking advantage of its own failure to comply with Community law.' In paragraph 48, on the other hand, the possibility of relying upon such a provision against an individual is excluded, inasmuch as a directive may not of itself impose obligations on an individual. In academic terminology, that means that where the period for their implementation has expired provisions of directives which from the point of view of their content are unconditional and sufficiently precise have 'vertical direct effect' but no 'horizontal direct effect.'

The reference for a preliminary ruling thus concerns the issue whether at the material time the BGC was 'the State' or 'an individual.'...

He summarised the legal status of BGC in the following terms:

...The BGC was a body with legal personality operating under the supervision of the authorities and having a monopoly on the supply of gas to homes and businesses in Great Britain. The members of the BGC were appointed by the Secretary of State, and he also determined their remuneration. ...The task of the BGC was to develop and maintain an efficient, co-ordinated and economical system of gas supply for Great Britain. ...The Secretary of State was empowered to require the BGC to report on its activities and, after laying that report before both Houses of Parliament, to give the BGC such directions as he considered appropriate on the basis of that report for the most efficient management of the undertaking. ... The Secretary of State could also, after consultation with the BGC, give the BGC general directions for the exercise and performance of its functions...

JUDGMENT

[16] As the Court has consistently held (see Case 8/81, *Becker v. Hauptzollamt Münster-Innenstadt*), where the Community authorities have, by means of a directive, placed member-States under a duty to adopt a certain course of action, the effectiveness of such a measure would be diminished if persons were prevented from relying upon it in proceedings before a court and national courts were prevented from taking it into consideration as an element of Community law. Consequently, a member-State which has not adopted the implementing measures required by the directive within the prescribed period may not plead, as against individuals, its own failure to perform the obligations which the directive entails. Thus, wherever the provisions of a directive appear, as far as their subject-matter is concerned, to be unconditional and sufficiently precise, those provisions may, in the absence of implementing measures adopted within the prescribed period, be relied upon as against any national provision which is incompatible with the directive or in so far as the provisions define rights which individuals are able to assert against the State.

[17] The Court further held in *Marshall*, at paragraph 49, that where a person is able to rely on a directive as against the State he may do so regardless of the capacity in which the latter is acting, whether as employer or as public authority. In either case it is necessary to prevent the State from taking advantage of its own failure to comply with Community law.

[18] On the basis of those considerations, the Court has held in a series of cases that unconditional and sufficiently precise provisions of a directive could be relied on against organisations or bodies which were subject to the authority or control of the State or had special powers beyond those which result from the normal rules applicable to relations between individuals.

[19] The Court has accordingly held that provisions of a directive could be relied on against tax authorities (Case 8/81, *Becker*, and 22 February 1990 in Case C-221/88, *ECSC v. Acciaierie E Ferriere Busseni*), local or regional authorities (Case 103/88, *Fratelli Costanzo v. Comune di Milano*), constitutionally independent authorities responsible for the maintenance of public order and safety (Case 222/84, *Johnston v. Chief Constable of the Royal Ulster Constabulary*), and public authorities providing public health services (Case 152/84, *Marshall*).

[20] It follows from the foregoing that a body, whatever its legal form, which has been made responsible, pursuant to a measure adopted by the State, for providing a public service under the control the State and has for that purpose special powers beyond those which result from the normal rules applicable in relations between individuals is included in any event among the bodies against which the provisions of a directive capable of having direct effect may be relied upon.

[21] With regard to Article 5(1) of Directive 76/207 it should be observed that in Case 152/84, *Marshall*, at paragraph 52, the Court held that that provision was

Decipher

The Tripartite Test is specified here.

unconditional and sufficiently precise to be relied on by an individual and to be applied by the national courts.

[22] The answer to the question referred by the House of Lords must therefore be that Article 5(1) of Council Directive 76/207 of 9 February 1976 may be relied upon in a claim for damages against a body, whatever its legal form, which has been made responsible, pursuant to a measure adopted by the State, for providing a public service under the control of the State and has for that purpose special powers beyond those which result from the normal rules applicable in relations between individuals.

In *Marshall* Miss Marshall had been able to bring her action because the Health Authority could be made out to be an organ of the state allowing for vertical direct effect. Given that there was no horizontal direct effect granted to directives the definable parameters of the state were clearly going to be of great importance. Not surprisingly the ECJ has taken an expansive definition of the state over the course of a number of cases. *Foster* is the seminal case in establishing the guidelines as to what ought to be seen as state, public body or emanation of the state.

In *Foster* it was fairly clear from the amount of state control over the BGC that the Court would have little difficulty assessing it as a public body. In subsequent cases it has gone on to include a privatised body within the definition (*Griffin v SW Water* [1995] IRLR 15) so that considering this purposive approach together with the availability of the bilateral (*National Union of Teachers v Governing Body of St Mary's Church of England School* [1997] CMLR 630) and *Kampelmann v Landschaftsverband Westfalen-Lippe* [1998] 1 CMLR 473 tests, the limits of what may now be seen as part of the state remain interestingly imprecise.

Sabine Von Colson and Elisabeth Kamann v Land Nordrhein-Westfalen Case 14/83 [1986] 2 CMLR 430

Panel: Martens de Wilmars CJ, Koopmans, Bahlmann and Galmot PPC, Pescatore, Lord Mackenzie Stuart, O'Keeffe, Bosco, Due, Everling and Kakouris JJ. Mme. Simone Rozès, Advocate-General

Legislation: Art 10 (ex Art 5); Directive 76/207

Facts: Two female plaintiffs applied for work as social workers at Werl prison in Germany. They were not appointed and the posts went to less well qualified male applicants. The German labour court established that this was a result of sex discrimination but that the Directive did not require any particular remedy to be available. In consequence the only penalty provided under German law amounted to damages for actual loss, that is, the reimbursement of transport expenses.

In a number of questions put to the ECJ the German court asked in essence for guidance as to what an appropriate sanction was in a case such as this.

As a side point note how the ECJ deals with the issue that although it was possible to see the prison service as a state emanation this case would have had difficulty passing the *van Gend en Loos* criteria in direct effect on the basis of the lack of clarity concerning the appropriate penalty – the very reason this case needed to be brought!

JUDGMENT

[21] In its fifth question the Arbeitsgericht essentially asks whether it is possible to infer from the directive any sanction in the event of discrimination other than the right to the conclusion of a contract of employment. Question 6 asks whether the directive, as properly interpreted, may be relied on before national courts by persons who have suffered injury.

[22] It is impossible to establish real equality of opportunity without an appropriate system of sanctions. That follows not only from the actual purpose of the directive but more specifically from Article 6 thereof which, by granting applicants for a post who have been discriminated against recourse to the courts, acknowledges that those candidates have rights of which they may avail themselves before the courts.

[23] Although, as has been stated in the reply to Question 1, full implementation of the directive does not require any specific form of sanction for unlawful discrimination, it does entail that that sanction be such as to guarantee real and effective judicial protection. Moreover it must also have a real deterrent effect on the employer. It follows that where a member-State chooses to penalise the breach of the prohibition of discrimination by the award of compensation, that compensation must in any event be adequate in relation to the damage sustained.

[24] In consequence it appears that national provisions limiting the right to compensation of persons who have been discriminated against as regards access to employment to a purely nominal amount, such as, for example, the reimbursement of expenses incurred by them in submitting their application, would not satisfy the requirements of an effective transposition of the directive. ...

[26] ... [T]he member-States' obligation arising from a directive to achieve the result envisaged by the directive and their duty under Article 5 of the Treaty to take all appropriate measures, whether general or particular, to ensure the fulfilment of that obligation, is binding on all the authorities of member-States including, for matters within their jurisdiction, the courts. It follows that, in applying the national law and in particular the provisions of a national law specifically introduced in order to implement Directive 76/207, national courts are required to interpret their national law in the light of the wording and the purpose of the directive in order to achieve the result referred to in Article 189(3).

[27] On the other hand, as the above considerations show, the directive does not include any unconditional and sufficiently precise obligation as regards sanctions for discrimination which, in the absence of implementing measures adopted in good time may be relied on by individuals in order to obtain specific compensation under the directive, where that is not provided for or permitted under national law.

[28] It should, however, be pointed out to the national court that although Directive 76/207/EEC, for the purpose of imposing a sanction for the breach of the prohibition of discrimination, leaves the member-States free to choose between the different solutions suitable for achieving its objective, it nevertheless requires that if a member-State chooses to penalise breaches of that prohibition by the award of compensation, then in order to ensure that it is effective and that it has a deterrent effect, that

Decipher

The Arbeitsgericht is the German labour court.

Decipher

The national courts as authorities of the Member States must comply with the Member States, obligation to fulfil a directives purpose.

compensation must in any event be adequate in relation to the damage sustained and must therefore amount to more than purely nominal compensation such as, for example, the reimbursement only of the expenses incurred in connection with the application. It is for the national court to interpret and apply the legislation adopted for the implementation of the directive in conformity with the requirements of Community law, in so far as it is given discretion to do so under national law.

 Alert

With regard to the concept of direct effect the ECJ seemed to have painted itself into a corner in that while an action based upon a directive could be brought, it could only be brought against a state, public body or emanation of the state. As seen in some earlier cases this left a rankling awareness of injustice among lawyers that employees of private concerns could not rely upon direct effect. This awareness goes some way to explaining the persistence of some Advocates-General who kept unsuccessfully pushing the ECJ in the direction of a finding in favour of horizontal direct effect (Lenz in *Faccini Dori*, Van Gervan in *Marshall 2*). *Von Colson* is the seminal case in establishing a different approach and a line of cases, which have gone some way to resolving the problem created by horizontality in direct effect.

Note however that the very last line of the judgment illuminates the limitation to the *Von Colson* principle and reveals the potential for uncertainty in its future applications. Because it is only an interpretive measure the courts can only interpret in conformity with Community law as far as the existing national law and language allow them. This led to problems in *Marleasing* [1992] 1 CMLR 305 (where the Spanish court ought not to have been able to create an EU amenable interpretation) which was not removed until the decision in *Wagner Miret* [1996] 1 CMLR 889.

As a final point it is worth noticing that the ECJ removed any potential for vertical and horizontal problems within the context of *Von Colson* in its decision in *Harz v Deutsche Tradax* [1986] 2 CMLR 430 where in almost identical circumstances a female employee of a private company was entitled to a similar redress.

2 State Liability

Andrea Francovich and Another v The Republic (Italy) Cases 6/90 & 9/90 [1993] 2 CMLR 66

Panel: Due CJ, Slynn, Joliet, Schockweiler, Grévisse and Kapteyn PPC, Mancini, Moitinho de Almeida, Rodríguez Iglesias, Díez de Velasco and Zuleeg JJ. M. Jean Mischo, Advocate-General

Legislation: Directive 80/987

Facts: Directive 80/987 sought to ensure that in the event of the bankruptcy of a company its employees would be able to claim their outstanding wages from a guarantee institution established by the Member States. The Italian state had failed to implement the Directive. Andrea Francovich had worked for an Italian company CDN Elletronica SnC which became bankrupt and from which he had been unable to claim his outstanding wages, even after court action. He therefore submitted that he was entitled to obtain from the Italian State the guarantees provided for by Directive

80/987 or, in the alternative, damages. Danila Bonifaci and 33 other employees brought a similar claim against the State for their outstanding wages owed by a separate company. The Italian courts concerned in these claims referred the question of whether a private individual affected by the failure of a member state to implement a directive could require the state to give effect to the directive and/or pay compensation for damage suffered.

ADVOCATE-GENERAL MISCHO

3. In the event of failure to implement a directive or its incorrect implementation, a member-State deprives Community law of the desired effect. It also commits a breach of Article 5 and Article 189(3) EEC, which affirm the binding nature of the directive and require the member-State to take all the measures necessary for its implementation.

4. Where the breach of that obligation is confirmed by a judgment of the Court of Justice delivered pursuant to Articles 169 to 171 EEC, the binding authority of a judicial decision and Article 171 EEC requires the member-State, which cannot raise any obstacle whatsoever, to take all appropriate measures to make good its default and give the desired effect to Community law. In so doing it may also be required to pay compensation for the harm which it has caused to individuals as a result of its unlawful conduct.

5. By virtue of Community law, it must be possible for the member-State to be held liable at least in cases where the conditions are met under which the Community incurs liability as a result of the breach of Community law by one of its institutions. In the case of a directive which should have been implemented by means of a legislative measure, it is therefore sufficient that the relevant provisions of the directive should have the purpose of protecting the interests of individuals. The condition of a sufficiently serious breach of a superior rule of law must be considered to have been met where the Court has declared the member-State in default in a judgment delivered under Articles 169 to 171.

The Court accepted the Advocate Generals reasoning but began its judgement by establishing that direct effect was not possible.

JUDGMENT

[1]...[E]ven though the provisions of the directive in question are sufficiently precise and unconditional as regards the determination of the persons entitled to the guarantee and as regards the content of that guarantee, those elements are not sufficient to enable individuals to rely on those provisions before the national courts. Those provisions do not identify the person liable to provide the guarantee, and the State cannot be considered liable on the sole ground that it has failed to take transposition measures within the prescribed period.

It then went on to give its judgement concerning state liability:

[31] It must be recalled first of all that the EEC Treaty has created its own legal system which is an integral part of the legal systems of the member-States and which their

courts are bound to apply; the subjects of that legal system are not only the member-States but also their nationals. Just as it imposes obligations on individuals, Community law is also intended to create rights which become part of their legal patrimony; those rights arise not only where they are expressly granted by the Treaty but also by virtue of obligations which the Treaty imposes in a clearly defined manner both on individuals and on the member-States and the Community institutions: see Case 26/62, *Van Gend en Loos* and Case 6/64, *Costa v. Enel.*

[32] Furthermore, it has been consistently held that the national courts whose task it is to apply the provisions of Community law in cases within their jurisdiction must ensure that those rules have full effect and protect the rights which they confer on individuals: see in particular Case 106/77, *Amministrazione delle Finanze dello Stato v. Simmenthal,* and Case C-213/89, *Factortame.*

[33] It must be held that the full effectiveness of Community rules would be impaired and the protection of the rights which they grant would be weakened if individuals were unable to obtain compensation when their rights are infringed by a breach of Community law for which a member-State can be held responsible.

[34] The possibility of compensation by the member-State is particularly indispensable where, as in this case, the full effectiveness of Community rules is subject to prior action on the part of the State and consequently individuals cannot, in the absence of such action, enforce the rights granted to them by Community law before the national courts.

[35] It follows that the principle of State liability for harm caused to individuals by breaches of Community law for which the State can be held responsible is inherent in the system of the Treaty.

[36] Further foundation for the obligation on the part of member-States to pay compensation for such harm is to be found in Article 5 EEC, under which the member-States are required to take all appropriate measures, whether general or particular, to ensure fulfilment of their obligations under Community law. Among these is the obligation to nullify the unlawful consequences of a breach of Community law: see, in relation to the analogous provision of Article 86 ECSC, Case 6/60, *Humblet v. Belgium.*

[37] It follows from all the foregoing that it is a principle of Community law that the member-States are obliged to pay compensation for harm caused to individuals by breaches of Community law for which they can be held responsible.

Alert

Having established that State liability was now an additional remedy to use against a recalcitrant Member State the ECJ stated the conditions under which the remedy would be available:

[39] Where, as in this case, a member-State fails to fulfil its obligations under Article 189(3) EEC to take all the measures necessary to achieve the result prescribed by a directive the full effectiveness of that rule of Community law requires that there should be a right to compensation where three conditions are met.

[40] The first of those conditions is that the result prescribed by the directive should entail the grant of rights to individuals. The second condition is that it should be possible to identify the content of those rights on the basis of the provisions of the directive. Finally, the third condition is the existence of a causal link between the breach of the State's obligation and the harm suffered by the injured parties.

[41] Those conditions are sufficient to give rise to a right on the part of individuals to obtain compensation, a right which is founded directly on Community law.

When a Member State failed to implement an EU measure the Commission, as the watchdog of the Treaty, could ultimately take action in the ECJ which could have resulted in a fine upon that State. This normally enforced the Treaty so far as the institutions were concerned but it did not resolve the ongoing problem of what to do when EU citizens suffered damage or loss when a malingering State failed to implement a directive. This provided the spur to the development of direct and indirect effect but what could be done if neither of these two routes failed to provide a solution?

Note that in *Frankovich* direct effect was not possible because the Directive lacked clarity about where exactly the money was coming from with which to pay the workers (see below) and indirect effect was not possible because of the absence of any national law capable of interpretation in line with the objectives of the directive. A double whammy prompting Advocate-General Mischo to begin his opinion by pointing out:

'Rarely has the Court been called upon to decide a case in which the adverse consequences for the individuals concerned of failure to implement a directive..[have been]… as shocking as in the case now before us'

The inequality that results when a Member State fails to comply with a directive affects not just the nationals of that state who lose out on their specific Treaty rights, but those other Member States which have complied with the directive often to their cost. Additionally such compliant States may well find their private companies are affected and no longer as competitive.

While *Francovich* established that at least individuals would obtain some redress in such a situation it left open the extent to which such an obligation could be pursued. A key question remained: did this ruling only apply where there was a total failure to implement a directive or did it apply to other EU law and if so, to what extent?

The following case went some way to addressing these questions.

Brasserie du Pecheur SA v Germany; R v Secretary of State for Transport exp Factortame Joined Cases 46 & 48/93 [1996] 1 CMLR 889

Panel: Rodríguez Iglesias (Rapporteur) P, Kakouris, Edward and Hirsch, PPC, Mancini, Schockweiler, Moitinho de Almeida, Gulmann and Murray, JJ. Sig. Giuseppe Tesauro, Advocate-General

Legislation: Art 34 (ex Art 28), Art 36 (ex Art 30), Art 59 (ex Art 52)

Facts: Brasserie du Pêcheur SA was a French brewery based at Schiltigheim (Alsace), which exported beer to Germany. These exports were stopped by the German government as they failed to comply with the German Reinheitsgebot (purity requirement). It was held that this prohibition was not compatible with Art 36 (ex Art 30). As a consequence Brasserie brought an action against the German government for compensation for the losses suffered to the amount of 1,800,000 DM.

In *Factortame 3*, Spanish fishermen challenged the compatibility of the UK Merchant Shipping Act 1988 with the Treaty. The registration requirement created by the Act imposed conditions concerning nationality, residence and domicile upon the owners of the fishing vessels that were found incompatible with Article 59 in *Factortame 2* [1990] 3 CMLR 1.

A number of questions were referred to the ECJ principally (for our purpose) of whether damages could be claimed where a Member State does not change a statute to comply with Community law (*Brasserie*) and whether damages could be claimed for all or any of the infringements of the Treaty committed against Factortame?

JUDGMENT

[18] The German, Irish and Netherlands Governments contend that Member States are required to make good loss or damage caused to individuals only where the provisions breached are not directly effective: in *Francovich and Others* the Court simply sought to fill a lacuna in the system for safeguarding rights of individuals. In so far as national law affords individuals a right of action enabling them to assert their rights under directly effective provisions of Community law, it is unnecessary, where such provisions are breached, also to grant them a right to reparation founded directly on Community law.

[19] That argument cannot be accepted.

[20] The Court has consistently held that the right of individuals to rely on the directly effective provisions of the Treaty before national courts is only a minimum guarantee and is not sufficient in itself to ensure the full and complete implementation of the Treaty (see, in particular, Case 168/85, *E.C. Commission v. Italy*, Case C-120/88, *E.C. Commission v. Italy* and C-119/89 *E.C. Commission v. Spain*. The purpose of that right is to ensure that provisions of Community law prevail over national provisions. It cannot, in every case, secure for individuals the benefit of the rights conferred on them by Community law and, in particular, avoid their sustaining damage as a result of a breach of Community law attributable to a Member State. As appears from paragraph [33] of the judgment in *Francovich and Others*, the full effectiveness of Community law would be impaired if individuals were unable to obtain redress when their rights were infringed by a breach of Community law.

[21] This will be so where an individual who is a victim of the non-transposition of a directive and is precluded from relying on certain of its provisions directly before the national court because they are insufficiently precise and unconditional, brings an action for damages against the defaulting Member State for breach of the third paragraph of Article 189 of the Treaty. In such circumstances, which obtained in the case of *Francovich* and Others, the purpose of reparation is to redress the injurious consequences of a Member State's failure to transpose a directive as far as beneficiaries of that directive are concerned.

[22] It is all the more so in the event of infringement of a right directly conferred by a Community provision upon which individuals are entitled to rely before the national courts. In that event, the right to reparation is the necessary corollary of the direct effect of the Community provision whose breach caused the damage sustained.

[23] In this case, it is undisputed that the Community provisions at issue, namely Article 30 of the Treaty in Case C-46/93 and Article 52 in Case C-48/93, have direct effect in the sense that they confer on individuals rights upon which they are entitled to rely directly before the national courts. Breach of such provisions may give rise to reparation...

State liability will be available where the criteria for direct effect fail to be made out. State liability will also be available where direct effect can be made out. In *Brasserie* and *Factortame 3* direct effect could be made out on the facts of each case.

[37] ...[T]he national courts ask the Court to specify the conditions under which a right to reparation of loss or damage caused to individuals by breaches of Community law attributable to a Member State is, in the particular circumstances, guaranteed by Community law.

[38] Although Community law imposes State liability, the conditions under which that liability gives rise to a right to reparation depend on the nature of the breach of Community law giving rise to the loss and damage (*Francovich and Others*).

[39] In order to determine those conditions, account should first be taken of the principles inherent in the Community legal order which form the basis for State liability, namely, first, the full effectiveness of Community rules and the effective protection of the rights which they confer and, second, the obligation to co-operate imposed on Member States by *Article 5* of the Treaty (*Francovich and Others*).

[40] In addition, as the Commission and the several governments which submitted observations have emphasised, it is pertinent to refer to the Court's case law on non-contractual liability on the part of the Community.

[41] First, the second paragraph of Article 215 of the Treaty refers, as regards the non-contractual liability of the Community, to the general principles common to the laws of the Member States, from which, in the absence of written rules, the Court also draws inspiration in other areas of Community law.

Decipher
The court includes general principles of EU among these sources.

[42] Second, the conditions under which the State may incur liability for damage caused to individuals by a breach of Community law cannot, in the absence of particular justification, differ from those governing the liability of the Community in like circumstances. The protection of the rights which individuals derive from Community law cannot vary depending on whether a national authority or a Community authority is responsible for the damage.

[43] The system of rules which the Court has worked out with regard to Article 215 of the Treaty, particularly in relation to liability for legislative measures, takes into account, *inter alia*, the complexity of the situations to be regulated, difficulties in the

application or interpretation of the texts and, more particularly, the margin of discretion available to the author of the act in question.

[44] Thus, in developing its case law on the non-contractual liability of the Community, in particular as regards legislative measures involving choices of economic policy, the Court has had regard to the wide discretion available to the institutions in implementing Community policies.

[45] The strict approach taken towards the liability of the Community in the exercise of its legislative activities is due to two considerations. First, even where the legality of measures is subject to judicial review, exercise of the legislative function must not be hindered by the prospect of actions for damages whenever the general interest of the Community requires legislative measures to be adopted which may adversely affect individual interests. Second, in a legislative context characterised by the exercise of a wide discretion, which is essential for implementing a Community policy, the Community cannot incur liability unless the institution concerned has manifestly and gravely disregarded the limits on the exercise of its powers. ... That said, the national legislature—like the Community institutions—does not systematically have a wide discretion when it acts in a field governed by Community law. Community law may impose upon it obligations to achieve a particular result or obligations to act or refrain from acting which reduce its margin of discretion, sometimes to a considerable degree. This is so, for instance, where, as in the circumstances to which the judgment in *Francovich and Others* relates, Article 189 of the Treaty places the Member State under an obligation to take, within a given period, all the measures needed in order to achieve the result required by a directive. In such a case, the fact that it is for the national legislature to take the necessary measures has no bearing on the Member State's liability for failing to transpose the directive.

[47] In contrast, where a Member State acts in a field where it has a wide discretion, comparable to that of the Community institutions in implementing Community policies, the conditions under which it may incur liability must, in principle, be the same as those under which the Community institutions incur liability in a comparable situation.

[48] In the case which gave rise to the reference in Case C-46/93, the German legislature had legislated in the field of foodstuffs, specifically beer. In the absence of Community harmonisation, the national legislature had a wide discretion in that sphere in laying down rules on the quality of beer put on the market.

[49] As regards the facts of Case C-48/93, the United Kingdom legislature also had a wide discretion. The legislation at issue was concerned, first, with the registration of vessels, a field which, in view of the state of development of Community law, falls within the jurisdiction of the Member States and, secondly, with regulating fishing, a sector in which implementation of the common fisheries policy leaves a margin of discretion to the Member States.

[50] Consequently, in each case the German and United Kingdom legislatures were faced with situations involving choices comparable to those made by the Community institutions when they adopt legislative measures pursuant to a Community policy.

Decipher

Note the argument here is that a EU institution would be liable where it has a wide discretion in how it may act only if it has excessively disregarded the limits of this discretion. This 'manifest and grave' formula will become part of its final decision and applied to Member States also.

Decipher

Again, a Member State must expect to be liable where a EU institution would be. A wide discretion must be manifestly and gravely exceeded.

Decipher

In both *Brasserie* and *Factortame 3* the States had a wide discretion.

[51] In such circumstances, Community law confers a right to reparation where three conditions are met: the rule of law infringed must be intended to confer rights on individuals; the breach must be sufficiently serious; and there must be a direct causal link between the breach of the obligation resting on the State and the damage sustained by the injured parties.

Alert

[52] First, those conditions satisfy the requirements of the full effectiveness of the rules of Community law and of the effective protection of the rights which those rules confer.

[53] Secondly, those conditions correspond in substance to those defined by the Court in relation to Article 215 in its case law on liability of the Community for damage caused to individuals by unlawful legislative measures adopted by its institutions.

[54] The first condition is manifestly satisfied in the case of Article 30 of the Treaty, the relevant provision in Case C-46/93, and in the case of Article 52, the relevant provision in Case C-48/93. Whilst Article 30 imposes a prohibition on Member States, it nevertheless gives rise to rights for individuals which the national courts must protect. Likewise, the essence of Article 52 is to confer rights on individuals.

[55] As to the second condition, as regards both Community liability under Article 215 and Member State liability for breaches of Community law, the decisive test for finding that a breach of Community law is sufficiently serious is whether the Member State or the Community institution concerned manifestly and gravely disregarded the limits on its discretion.

[56] The factors which the competent court may take into consideration include the clarity and precision of the rule breached, the measure of discretion left by that rule to the national or Community authorities, whether the infringement and the damage caused was intentional or involuntary, whether any error of law was excusable or inexcusable, the fact that the position taken by a Community institution may have contributed towards the omission, and the adoption or retention of national measures or practices contrary to Community law.

Alert

[57] On any view, a breach of Community law will clearly be sufficiently serious if it has persisted despite a judgment finding the infringement in question to be established, or a preliminary ruling or settled case law of the Court on the matter from which it is clear that the conduct in question constituted an infringement.

An inevitable consequence of any ground breaking legal decision is a degree of opaqueness about how far the newly created obligation extends. Milestone as it was, *Francovich* attracted the same problem. It was a decision about a Member State's total failure to implement a Directive. Did this apply to other EU measures? Did it apply to a partial failure to implement a directive? *Brasserie du Pecheur/Factortame 3* addressed these issues by providing a formulaic set of conditions which can be used to deal with a wider range of factors such as partial breaches as opposed to the total breach situation in *Francovich*. The requirement that a breach needs to be sufficiently serious to be actionable is the effective difference between the *Francovich* criteria and those laid out in this case. Subsequent case law has gone on to illustrate and refine State liability further. In this context note *Dillenkofer* [1996] 3 CMLR 469.

This involved the non-implementation of a Directive very similar to that in *Francovich*. Here the court did not need to invoke the *Brasserie* conditions, simply deciding that the non-implementation by the German government was sufficiently serious in its own right.

Conclusion

The Treaty allowed the Commission to enforce obligations by fines imposed upon Member States which failed to fulfil their obligations. However, there was nothing in the original Treaty which allowed redress for individuals in their national courts. While the development of the concepts seen in this Chapter have gone a long way to making up for this defect in the Treaty it is true that there are still many gaps through which an individual action may fall. The lack of horizontal direct effect pushes the employees of private companies outside the shelter of *van Gend en Loos*. The lack of national law or the opportunity to provide the correct interpretation of it removes indirect effect. A failure to make out one of the factors in paragraph 56 of *Brasserie* would defeat State liability. In conclusion, despite the cumulative nature of the potential remedies, a private individual could still find no remedy covering their particular situation.

Further Reading

Drake, Sara; '20 Years After Von Colson: the Impact of 'indirect effect' on the Protection of the Individuals Community Rights' (2005) 30 ELR 329

Fairhurst, John; *Law of the European Union*. Longman/Pearson 7th ed, p280

Granger, MPF; 'National Application of Francovich and the Construction of a European Administrative Jus Commune' (2007) 32 ELR 157

Horspool and Humphreys; *European Union Law*. 4th ed, OUP, Chapters 7 and 8

Nassimdian, Dimitra; 'And We Keep on Meeting: (De)fragmenting State Liability' (2007) 32 ELR 819

Steiner and Woods; *EU Law*. 10th ed, OUP, Chapters 5 and 9

'The Evolution of the European legal order.' (2004) CMLR 303

Article 101 –
Anti-Competitive
Agreements

Topic List

Chris Garside

Introduction

Competition law plays an important role in maintaining the proper function of the common market. The aim of the legislation is to prevent companies acting in a collusive manner or abusing a dominant position to the detriment of other businesses and consumers.

The legislative framework in the UK is as follows: Art 101 (ex Art 81) and Art 102 (ex Art 82) set out the law applicable on an EU wide basis and any purported breach with a cross border element will be investigated under this legislation. The UK has enacted the Competition Act 1998 and the Enterprise Act 2002. A purported breach within the UK only will be investigated under this legislation. The provisions of Arts 101 and 102 are mirrored in the Competition Act 1998.

Since the introduction of the Modernisation Regulation (Reg 1/2003) the majority of investigations that do not have a cross-border element will fall to be investigated by the National Competition Authorities ("NCAs") (the Office of Fair Trading and the UK Competition Commission in the UK). Therefore, investigations by the Commission under Arts 101 and 102 are now the exception rather than the rule.

Appeals of decisions of the NCAs are heard in national courts of the Member States (the Competition Appeal Tribunal, the Court of Appeal and the Supreme Court in the UK). However, all such decisions must be compatible with the decisions of the CFI and the ECJ as well as EU legislation.

The Commission and NCAs in each Member State enjoy extensive powers to investigate and issue penalties to undertakings. Appeals by parties of the decisions of the Commission have led to a detailed examination of all parts of Arts 101 and 102 over the years. On the whole this examination has taken place within the CFI and ECJ, which hear appeals from undertakings on decisions of the Commission.

Jurisprudence relating to Art 101 is considered in this Chapter. The next Chapter will deal with jurisprudence relating to Art 102.

All the judgements contained within this chapter result from appeals of decisions of the Commission and the majority were heard before the introduction of the Modernisation Regulation. Accordingly, they are all judgements of the CFI and the ECJ. The case law of the national courts is not considered in this text and is outside the scope of this course.

1   Agreements, Decisions and Concerted Practices

By its nature anti-competitive behaviour is often established in an informal fashion. However, there are also many circumstances in which undertakings do formally document their intentions. In drafting Art 101, the Commission tried to ensure that all forms of collusive behaviour between undertakings which could distort competition, whether formally or informally documented, were prohibited. For this reason Art 101 identifies three different types of collusion - agreement between undertakings, decisions by associations of undertakings and concerted practices.

Commission v ANIC Partecipazioni SpA Case 49/92P [2001] 4 CMLR 17

Panel: Kapteyn PC, Hirsc, Mancini (Rapporteur), Murray and Ragnemalm JJ. Georgios Cosmas, Advocate-General

Legislation: Art 101 (ex Art 81)

Facts: The Commission made an initial decision that a number of undertakings in the polypropylene market had for some time met regularly in secret meetings and put in place a number of measures to control prices and allocate market share over a long period of time.

JUDGMENT

102 By its fourth plea in law, ANIC criticises the Court of First Instance for having wrongly rejected its complaint that the infringement had not been legally characterised as either an agreement or a concerted practice within the meaning of Article 81 of the Treaty.

103 First, the Court of First Instance has not clearly indicated the actual criteria for characterising the type of infringement. Moreover, its classification does not correspond to the distinction made by the Commission in its decision, which uses the concept of concerted practice as a catch-all device for preventing suspected infringements from going unpunished, in the absence of proof of common intention between the producers. According to ANIC, the distinction between an agreement and a concerted practice has consequences for the level of proof required of the Commission and therefore for the rights of defence of the parties. The Commission's line of argument would lead to the conclusion that the reference to agreements in Article 81 of the Treaty is superfluous. If a concerted practice could consist in the mental element alone, with no need for any physical element, the two concepts would become redundant and would differ only as to the degree of manifestation of intention, joint intention in the case of an agreement and the manifestation of unilateral intention in the case of a concerted practice. ...

105 Thirdly, ANIC states that the characterisation of the alleged cartel as a single infringement, treated as an agreement and concerted practice, may have dangerous legal consequences. In particular it led in this case to the grouping together, as a 'single' infringement, of the various lines of conduct followed by 15 undertakings over a period of approximately five years and prevented infringements which could actually be ascribed to an individual undertaking from being distinguished from those alleged.

106 Fourthly, ANIC complains that the Court of First Instance accepted the Commission's dual characterisation of the infringement as an agreement and concerted practice. ANIC considers that such a characterisation alters the burden of proof for the Commission and, consequently, the thrust of the defence mounted by the undertaking concerned...

107 The Commission states that this plea is based on a supposed difference in the burden of proof according to whether the infringement is a concerted practice or an agreement. That supposed difference is wrongly based on a literal construction of the term `concerted practice', according to which `practice' refers to conduct on the market and, consequently, to an objectively observable element. Such a construction is contrary to the ratio legis which bolsters the prohibition by widening it to cover concerting arrangements that are less elaborate than a real agreement, so as to prevent the rule being too easily circumvented. ANIC's argument would paradoxically weaken the prohibition, by requiring more exacting proof for a concerted practice than for an agreement. Article 81 of the Treaty would thus be disarmed in relation to concerted practices since, contrary to what counts for agreements, only the anti-competitive effect would count, not the object.

108 The list in Article 81of the Treaty is intended to apply to all collusion between undertakings, whatever the form it takes. There is continuity between the cases listed. The only essential thing is the distinction between independent conduct, which is allowed, and collusion, which is not, regardless of any distinction between types of collusion. ANIC's argument would break down the unity and generality of the prohibited phenomenon and would remove from the ambit of the prohibition, without any reason, certain types of collusion which are no less dangerous than others. The Court of First Instance rightly rejected that argument at paragraph 199 of the judgment when it referred to the mental element without requiring an observable physical element.

109 The Court observes first of all that, at paragraphs 198 and 202 of the contested judgment, the Court of First Instance held that the Commission was entitled to categorise as agreements certain types of conduct on the part of the undertakings concerned, and, in the alternative, as concerted practices certain other forms of conduct on the part of the same undertakings. At paragraph 204, the Court of First Instance held that ANIC had taken part in an integrated set of schemes constituting a single infringement which progressively manifested itself in both unlawful agreements and unlawful concerted practices. ...

111 At paragraph 205, the Court of First Instance held that the Commission was entitled to characterise that single infringement as `an agreement and a concerted practice', since the infringement involved at one and the same time factual elements to be characterised as `agreements' and factual elements to be characterised as `concerted practices' within the meaning of Article 81 of the Treaty. According to the Court of First Instance, given such a complex infringement, the dual characterisation by the Commission in Art. 1 of the Polypropylene Decision had to be understood not as requiring, simultaneously and cumulatively, proof that each of those factual elements presented the constituent elements both of an agreement and of a concerted practice, but rather as referring to a complex whole comprising a number of factual elements some of which were characterised as agreements and others as concerted practices for the purposes of Article 81 of the Treaty, which lays down no specific category for a complex infringement of this type.

112 Secondly, it must be observed that, if Article 81 of the Treaty distinguishes between `concerted practices', `agreements between undertakings' and `decisions by associations of undertakings', the aim is to have the prohibitions of that Article catch different forms of coordination and collusion between undertakings (see, to that effect, in particular, Imperial Chemical Industries Ltd. v Commission of the European Communitie s(Case 48/69).

113 It does not, however, follow that patterns of conduct having the same anti-competitive object, each of which, taken in isolation, would fall within the meaning of `agreement', `concerted practice' or `a decision by an association of undertakings', cannot constitute different manifestations of a single infringement of Article 81 of the Treaty.

114 The Court of First Instance was therefore entitled to consider that patterns of conduct by several undertakings were a manifestation of a single and complex infringement, corresponding partly to an agreement and partly to a concerted practice.

115 Thirdly, it must be borne in mind that a concerted practice, within the meaning of Article 81 of the Treaty, refers to a form of coordination between undertakings which, without having been taken to a stage where an agreement properly so called has been concluded, knowingly substitutes for the risks of competition practical cooperation between them...

116 The Court of Justice has further explained that criteria of coordination and cooperation must be understood in the light of the concept inherent in the provisions of the Treaty relating to competition, according to which each economic operator must determine independently the policy which he intends to adopt on the market (see (Case 40/73) Suiker Unie v. Commission).

117 According to that case-law, although that requirement of independence does not deprive economic operators of the right to adapt themselves intelligently to the existing and anticipated conduct of their competitors, it does however strictly preclude any direct or indirect contact between such operators, the object or effect whereof is either to influence the conduct on the market of an actual or potential competitor or to disclose to such a competitor the course of conduct which they themselves have decided to adopt or contemplate adopting on the market, where the object or effect of such contact is to create conditions of competition which do not correspond to the normal conditions of the market in question, regard being had to the nature of the products or services offered, the size and number of the undertakings and the volume of the said market.

118 It follows that, as is clear from the very terms of Article 81 of the Treaty, a concerted practice implies, besides undertakings' concerting together, conduct on the market pursuant to those collusive practices, and a relationship of cause and effect between the two. ...

132 It follows that, whilst the concepts of an agreement and of a concerted practice have partially different elements, they are not mutually incompatible. Contrary to ANIC's allegations, the Court of First Instance did not therefore have to require the

Commission to categorise either as an agreement or as a concerted practice each form of conduct found but was right to hold that the Commission had been entitled to characterise some of those forms of conduct as principally `agreements' and others as `concerted practices'.

The ECJ has interpreted the terms "agreement" and "decision" widely. Accordingly any agreement whether oral or written and whether imposing legally or only morally binding obligations is likely to be capable of constituting collusion. Equally, any decision of associations of undertaking, even if not binding upon the members of the association, may constitute collusion.

The term "concerted practice" has provided more food for thought than the terms "agreement" and "decision". The reason is simple: the term "concerted practice" is intended to sweep up the forms of collusive behaviour which do not constitute an agreement between undertakings or a decision by an association of undertakings. It is therefore likely to be a less formal type of arrangement. However, because of a lack of certainty as to the form of the collusion where a concerted practice is suspected the ECJ has to be careful not to confuse behaviour which is normal in a particular market with collusive behaviour.

The nature of a concerted practice came to be discussed by the ECJ in detail in the following case.

Imperial Chemical Industries Ltd. v Commission of the European Communities Case 48/69 [1972] CMLR 557 ('Dyestuffs')

Panel: R. Lecourt P, Mertens de Wilmars, H. Kutscher, A. M. Donner, A. Trabucchi, R. Monaco and P. Pescatore JJ. Monsieur Henri Mayras, Advocate-General

Legislation: Art 101 (ex Art 81)

Facts: A subsidiary of Imperial Chemical Industries Ltd ("ICI") within the EU increased the price of a bleaching agent. This led the Commission to investigate allegations of concerted practices within the dyestuffs industry. Investigations found that the remainder of the competitors in the same market increased their respective prices within a short space of time and by the same margin as each other. Similar price increases occurred on three separate occasions in 1964, 1965 and 1967.

JUDGMENT

64 Article 81 draws a distinction between the concept of "concerted practices" and that of "agreements between undertakings" or of "decisions by associations of undertakings"; the object is to bring within the prohibition of that Art. a form of coordination between undertakings which, without having reached the stage where an agreement properly so-called has been concluded, knowingly substitutes practical cooperation between them for the risks of competition.

65 By its very nature, then, a concerted practice does not have all the elements of a contract but may inter alia arise out of coordination which becomes apparent from the behaviour of the participants .

66 Although parallel behaviour may not by itself be identified with a concerted practice, it may however amount to strong evidence of such a practice if it leads to conditions of competition which do not correspond to the normal conditions of the market, having regard to the nature of the products, the size and number of the undertakings, and the volume of the said market.

67 This is especially the case if the parallel conduct is such as to enable those concerned to attempt to stabilize prices at a level different from that to which competition would have led, and to consolidate established positions to the detriment of effective freedom of movement of the products in the common market and of the freedom of consumers to choose their suppliers.

68 Therefore the question whether there was a concerted action in this case can only be correctly determined if the evidence upon which the contested decision is based is considered, not in isolation, but as a whole, account being taken of the specific features of the market in the products in question.

The characteristic features of the market in dyestuffs

69 The market in dyestuffs is characterized by the fact that 80 per cent of the market is supplied by about ten producers, very large ones in the main, which often manufacture these products together with other chemical products or pharmaceutical specialities.

70 The production patterns and therefore the cost structures of these manufacturers are very different and this makes it difficult to ascertain competing manufacturers' costs.

71 The total number of dyestuffs is very high, each undertaking producing more than a thousand.

72 The average extent to which these products can be replaced by others, is considered relatively good for standard dyes, but it can be very low or even non-existent for speciality dyes.

73 As regards speciality products, the market tends in certain cases towards an oligopolistic situation.

74 Since the price of dyestuffs forms a relatively small part of the price of the final product of the user undertaking, there is little elasticity of demand for dyestuffs on the market as a whole and this encourages price increases in the short term.

75 Another factor is that the total demand for dyestuffs is constantly increasing, and this tends to induce producers to adopt a policy enabling them to take advantage of this increase.

76 In the territory of the community, the market in dyestuffs in fact consists of five separate national markets with different price levels which cannot be explained by differences in costs and charges affecting producers in those countries.

77 Thus the establishment of the common market would not appear to have had any effect on this situation, since the differences between national price levels have scarcely decreased.

Alert

78 On the contrary, it is clear that each of the national markets has the characteristics of an oligopoly and that in most of them price levels are established under the influence of a "priceleader", who in some cases is the largest producer in the country concerned, and in other cases is a producer in another member state or a third state, acting through a subsidiary. ...

88 In 1964 all the undertakings in question announced their increases and immediately put them into effect, the initiative coming from Ciba-Italy which, on 7 January 1964, following instructions from Ciba-Switzerland, announced and immediately introduced an increase of 15 per cent. This initiative was followed by the other producers on the Italian market within two or three days.

89 On 9 January ICI Holland took the initiative in introducing the same increase in the Netherlands, whilst on the same day Bayer took the same initiative on the Belgo-Luxembourg market.

[The Court went on to consider two further rounds of price increases in 1965 and 1967].

...

99 Viewed as a whole, the three consecutive increases reveal progressive cooperation between the undertakings concerned.

100 In fact, after the experience of 1964, when the announcement of the increases and their application coincided, although with minor differences as regards the range of products affected, the increases of 1965 and 1967 indicate a different mode of operation.

Here, the undertakings taking the initiative, BASF and Geiger respectively, announced their intentions of making an increase some time in advance, which allowed the undertakings to observe each other's reactions on the different markets, and to adapt themselves accordingly.

101 By means of these advance announcements the various undertakings eliminated all uncertainty between them as to their future conduct and, in doing so, also eliminated a large part of the risk usually inherent in any independent change of conduct on one or several markets.

Alert

102 This was all the more the case since these announcements, which led to the fixing of general and equal increases in prices for the markets in dyestuffs, rendered the market transparent as regard the percentage rates of increase.

103 Therefore, by the way in which they acted, the undertakings in question temporarily eliminated with respect to prices some of the preconditions for competition on the market which stood in the way of the achievement of parallel uniformity of conduct.

Alert

104 The fact that this conduct was not spontaneous is corroborated by an examination of other aspects of the market.

105 In fact, from the number of producers concerned it is not possible to say that the European market in dyestuffs is, in the strict sense, an oligopoly in which price competition could no longer play a substantial role.

106 These producers are sufficiently powerful and numerous to create a considerable risk that in times of rising prices some of them might not follow the general movement but might instead try to increase their share of the market by behaving in an individual way.

107 Furthermore, the dividing-up of the common market into five national markets with different price levels and structures makes it improbable that a spontaneous and equal price increase would occur on all the national markets. ...

109 Therefore, although parallel conduct in respect of prices may well have been an attractive and risk-free objective for the undertakings concerned, it is hardly conceivable that the same action could be taken spontaneously at the same time, on the same national markets and for the same range of products.

110 Nor is it any more plausible that the increases of January 1964, introduced on the Italian market and copied on the Netherlands and Belgo-Luxembourg markets which have little in common with each other either as regards the level of prices or the pattern of competition, could have been brought into effect within a period of two or three days without prior concertation.

111 As regards the increases of 1965 and 1967 concertation took place openly, since all the announcements of the intention to increase prices with effect from a certain date and for a certain range of products made it possible for producers to decide on their conduct regarding the special cases of France and Italy.

112 In proceeding in this way, the undertakings mutually eliminated in advance any uncertainties concerning their reciprocal behaviour on the different markets and thereby also eliminated a large part of the risk inherent in any independent change of conduct on those markets.

113 The general and uniform increase on those different markets can only be explained by a common intention on the part of those undertakings, first, to adjust the level of prices and the situation resulting from competition in the form of discounts, and secondly, to avoid the risk, which is inherent in any price increase, of changing the conditions of competition.

The decision of the ECJ in *Dyestuffs* can be contrasted with the decision of the ECJ in the next case in which the ECJ found that the pricing decisions were found to be a normal feature of the market.

Ahlström Osakeyhtiö and others v Commission of the European Communities **Cases 89,104,114,116-117 & 125-129/85 Joined Cases 89/85 [1988] 4 CMLR 901 (the** *"Wood Pulp Cartel"* **case)**

Panel: Lord Mackenzie Stuart CJ; Bosco, Due, Moitinho de Almeida and Rodriguez Iglesias PPC; Koopmans, Everling, Bahlmann, Galmot, Kakouris, Joliet, O'Higgins and Schockweiler JJ. M. Marco Darmon, Advocate General

Legislation: Art 101 (ex Art 81)

Facts: The Commission investigated allegations of concerted practices by a large number of wood pulp producers suspecting that the producers were colluding to co-ordinate price changes.

JUDGMENT

126...[In] this case, concertation is not the only plausible explanation for the parallel conduct. To begin with, the system of price announcements may be regarded as constituting a rational response to the fact that the pulp market constituted a long-term market and to the need felt by both buyers and sellers to limit commercial risks. Further, the similarity in the dates of price announcements may be regarded as a direct result of the high degree of market transparency, which does not have to be described as artificial. Finally, the parallelism of prices and the price trends may be satisfactorily explained by the oligopolistic tendencies of the market and by the specific circumstances prevailing in certain periods. Accordingly, the parallel conduct established by the Commission does not constitute evidence of concertation.

127 In the absence of a firm, precise and consistent body of evidence, it must be held that concertation regarding announced prices has not been established by the Commission. Art 1(1) of the contested decision must therefore be annulled.

2   Effect on Trade between Member States

Collusive behaviour will fall within the prohibition contained in Art 101 if it may affect trade between member states. As the ECJ set out in *Société Technique Minière v Maschinenbau Ulm GmbH* [1966] CMLR 357 (the *"STM"* case) the mere potential to affect trade is sufficient.

The decision of the ECJ in *Brasserie de Haecht SA v Wilkin-Janssen* Case 3/67 [1968] CMLR 26 provided that the cumulative effect of a number of small agreements within even one single Member State could have the potential to effect trade between Member States. However, it is important when analysing any agreement between undertakings which have less than 10-15% share of the relevant market may be considered de minimus under the Notice on Agreements of Minor Importance [2001] OJ C368/13.

2.1 The object or effect of prevention, restriction or distortion of competition

Collusive behaviour, which has, as its object or effect the prevention, restriction or distortion of competition is capable of falling within the prohibition contained within Article 101. Both horizontal and vertical agreements are capable of having as their object or effect the prevention, restriction or distortion of competition.

The terms "object" and "effect" are provided in the alternative and it is only necessary to show one or the other. As a result, the mere intention to distort competition may be enough even if an undertaking is not successful in its aims. The ECJ discussed this point in *STM*.

Société Technique Minière ("STM") v Maschinenbau Ulm GmbH ("MBU") Case 32/65 [1966] CMLR 357 (the "STM" case),

Panel: L. Hammes CJ, L. Delvaux, A. M. Donner, A. Trabucchi, R. Lecourt JJ. Herr Karl Roemer, Advocate-General

Legislation: Art 101 (ex Art 81)

Facts: STM held an exclusive supply contract with an exclusive right to sell in France equipment produced by MBU. The contract contained an agreement by STM not to sell their competing equipment in France and MBU also agreed not to compete with STM in France. However, as MBU's contract with STM and its contract with other distributors did not prevent the selling of MBU equipment into other countries the companies did not have protection within their territory against another MBU distributor selling into that country. As a result STM was unhappy about the contract and so argued that it was invalid under Art 101.

JUDGMENT

Finally, for the agreement at issue to be caught by the prohibition contained in Article 81 it must have as its 'object or effect the prevention, restriction or distortion of competition within the common market'.

The fact that these are not cumulative but alternative requirements, indicated by the conjunction 'or', leads first to the need to consider the precise purpose of the agreement, in the economic context in which it is to be applied. This interference with competition referred to in Article 81 must result from all or some of the clauses of the agreement itself. Where, however, an analysis of the said clauses does not reveal the effect on competition to be sufficiently deleterious, the consequences of the agreement should then be considered and for it to be caught by the prohibition it is then necessary to find that those factors are present which show that competition has in fact been prevented or restricted or distorted to an appreciable extent.

If matters are not clear from the object of an agreement, the NCA's must apply a logical methodology in deciding whether the effect of an agreement is in fact to prevent, restrict or distort competition. The ECJ discussed the requirements of this methodology in the following case.

European Night Services v Commission Cases T-374, 375, 384, 388/94 [1998] 5 CMLR 718

Panel: Kalogeropoulos P, Bellamy, and Pirrung JJ

Legislation Art 101 (ex Art 81)

Facts: Four rail companies, including British Rail, established European Night Services ("ENS") to operate overnight rail services through the channel tunnel from the UK and into continental Europe. The agreement was found by the Commission to breach Art 101 unless stringent conditions were adhered to. ENS argued that the Commission has failed to give sufficient reasons as to why the agreement breached Art 101 and so the case was referred to the CFI.

JUDGMENT

136 Before any examination of the parties' arguments as to whether the Commission's analysis as regards restrictions of competition was correct, it must be borne in mind that in assessing an agreement under Article 81 of the Treaty, account should be taken of the actual conditions in which it functions, in particular the economic context in which the undertakings operate, the products or services covered by the agreement and the actual structure of the market concerned …

137 It must also be stressed that the examination of conditions of competition is based not only on existing competition between undertakings already present on the relevant market but also on potential competition, in order to ascertain whether, in the light of the structure of the market and the economic and legal context within which it functions, there are real concrete possibilities for the undertakings concerned to compete among themselves or for a new competitor to penetrate the relevant market and compete with the undertakings already established… .

Therefore the methodology of the NCAs should be to undertake an analysis of the relevant product and geographical market in which the behaviour operates together with any other relevant features of the particular market in question to establish whether the collusive behaviour has in fact had an anti-competitive effect.

2.2 The Prevention, Restriction or Distortion of Competition

Article 101(1) sets out at paragraphs (a) to (e) a non-exhaustive list of agreements, decisions and concerted practices which are prohibited. The list is illustrative only and any type of collusive behaviour is generally likely to be capable of falling within the prohibition of Article 101(1) if the pattern of competition within the relevant market differs as a result of the collusive behaviour.

3 Defences

3.1 The Article 101(3) Defence

In some cases it will be clear that collusive behaviour is made up only of anti-competitive elements. For instance, an agreement between two undertakings to fix a tender process is unlikely to be viewed as anything other than a blatant distortion of competition. However, the NCAs and the courts face more difficulties where arrangements between undertakings contain both competitive and anti-competitive elements. Such agreements can in certain circumstances not threaten competition within the common market and they may actually assist competition. This is recognised in Art 101(3) which dis-applies the prohibition contained within Art 101(1) in respect of such agreements.

Since the introduction of Regulation 1/2003 an undertaking may decide that an agreement falls within Art 101(3) by looking at the individual circumstances in which that agreement operates. Alternatively an undertaking may decide that the agreement is exempt as it falls within a block exemption issued by the Commission. However, if the view of that undertaking is challenged by the NCAs it is necessary for the court to apply a methodology in deciding whether the agreement does properly fall within Art 101(3).

The methodology the CFI and ECJ apply was developed before the introduction of Regulation 1/2003 and essentially consists of the court carrying out a balancing act between the pro-competitive and anti-competitive effects of the agreement (sometimes referred to as the Rule of Reason). The development of the methodology can be seen in *STM* and the following case.

Société Technique Minière ("STM") v Maschinenbau Ulm GmbH ("MBU") Case 39/65 [1966] CMLR 357

Facts: See earlier for the facts of this case.

JUDGMENT

The competition in question must be understood within the actual context in which it would occur in the absence of the agreement in dispute. In particular it may be doubted whether there is an interference with competition if the said agreement seems really necessary for the penetration of a new area by an undertaking. Therefore, in order to decide whether an agreement containing a clause 'granting an exclusive right of sale' is to be considered as prohibited by reason of its object or of its effect, it is appropriate to take into account in particular the nature and quantity, limited or otherwise, of the products covered by the agreement, the position and importance of the grantor and the concessionaire on the market for the products concerned, the isolated nature of the disputed agreement or, alternatively, its position in a series of agreements, the severity of the clauses intended to protect the exclusive dealership or, alternatively, the opportunities allowed for other commercial competitors in the same products by way of parallel re-exportation and importation .

Pronuptia de Paris GmbH v Pronuptia de Paris Irmgard Schillgallis **Case 161/84 [1986] 1 CMLR 414**

Panel: Lord Mackenzie Stuart CJ, Everling, Bahlmann and Joliet PPC, Koopmans, Due and Galmot JJ. Mr. Pieter Verloren Van Themaat, Advocate-General

Legislation Art 101 (ex Art 81)

Facts: A dispute arose in the German courts between a franchisor and franchisee concerning their agreement for the distribution of wedding dresses and other articles sold under the Pronuptia de Paris trademark. The German court asked the ECJ whether the franchise agreement infringed Art 101.

JUDGMENT

(1) the compatibility of franchise agreements for the distribution of goods with Article 81 depends on the provisions contained therein and on their economic context.

(2) provisions which are strictly necessary in order to ensure that the know-how and assistance provided by the franchisor do not benefit competitors do not constitute restrictions of competition for the purposes of Article 81.

(3) provisions which establish the control strictly necessary for maintaining the identity and reputation of the network identified by the common name or symbol do not constitute restrictions of competition for the purposes of Article 81.

(4) provisions which share markets between the franchisor and the franchisees or between franchisees constitute restrictions of competition for the purposes of Article 81(1).

(5) the fact that the franchisor makes price recommendations to the franchisee does not constitute a restriction of competition, so long as there is no concerted practice between the franchisor and the franchisees or between the franchisees themselves for the actual application of such prices.

(6) franchise agreements for the distribution of goods which contain provisions sharing markets between the franchisor and the franchisees or between franchisees are capable of affecting trade between member states.

It is unclear whether the methodology will change significantly following the introduction of Regulation 1/2003.

3.2 The De Minimis Defence

An undertaking may also be able to able to avoid the prohibition contained within Article 101(1) if it can demonstrate that the agreement does not have an appreciable effect on either competition or inter-state trade (the de-minimis defence). The defence was introduced in the judgment of the ECJ in *Volk v Vervaecke* Case 5/69 [1969] CMLR 273.

Volk v Vervaecke Case 5/69 [1969] CMLR 273

Panel: R. Lecourt P, A. Trabucchi, Mertens de Wilmars, A. M. Donner, W. Strauss, R. Monaco and P. Pescatore JJ. M. Joseph Gand, Advocate-General

Legislation: Art 101 (ex Art 81)

Facts: Mr Volk was the owner of Erd & Co which manufactured washing machines and of Vervaecke which manufactured electrical appliances. Both were small companies. Vervaecke held exclusive rights to sell Volk's products in Belgium and Luxemburg. The German courts asked the Community Court (the predecessor to the ECJ) whether the agreement breached Art 101 considering the small market shares of the parties.

JUDGMENT

...The question is thus reduced to whether, in deciding whether such agreements fall within the prohibition set out in Article 81 of the treaty, regard must be had to the proportion of the market which the grantor controls or endeavours to obtain in the territory ceded.

If an agreement is to be capable of affecting trade between member states it must be possible to foresee with a sufficient degree of probability on the basis of a set of objective factors of law or of fact that the agreement in question may have an influence, direct or indirect, actual or potential, on the pattern of trade between member states in such a way that it might hinder the attainment of the objectives of a single market between states. Moreover, the prohibition in Article 81 is applicable only if the agreement in question also has as its object or effect, the prevention, restriction or distortion of competition within the common market. Those conditions must be understood by reference to the actual circumstances of the agreement. Consequently an agreement falls outside the prohibition in Article 81 when it has only an insignificant effect on the markets, taking into account the weak position which, the persons concerned have on the market of the product in question. Thus an exclusive dealing agreement, even with absolute territorial protection, may, having regard to the weak position of the persons concerned on the market in the products in question in the area covered by the absolute protection, escape the prohibition laid down in Article 81.

The principle developed in Volk is now enshrined in the Notice on Agreements of Minor Importance [2001] OJ C368/13. However, it should be noted that this Notice contains a prohibition on certain hardcore restrictions so that, no matter what the market share of the undertakings certain agreements, such as fixing prices, are not exempted by the Notice.

Further reading

van Gerven, G and Varona, E: 'The Wood Pulp Case and the Future of Concerted Practices' (1994) 31 CMLRev 575

Robertson, Beverly: 'What is a restriction of competition? The implications of the CFIs judgment in O2 Germany and the rule of reason' ECLR 2007

Article 102 – Abuse of a Dominant Position

Topic List

Chris Garside

Introduction: Anti-Competitive Agreements

The previous Chapter reviewed how the ECJ and CFI have applied Art 101 (ex Art 81), which seeks to deal with the threat to competition posed by collusive behaviour. This Chapter contains a review the treatment by the ECJ and CFI of those cases involving a breach of Art 102 (ex Art 82), which seeks to deal with the abuse by an undertaking of a dominant position.

It is important to remember that dominance in itself is not prohibited as this dominance may be a reflection of a successful and efficient company. For instance most people would suspect that Microsoft Corp. ("Microsoft") is dominant in several markets, for instance the market for home PC operating systems. The Commission has indeed found that Microsoft is dominant in several markets. However, it is only when the Commission has found that Microsoft has abused that dominance that it has faced penalties under the EU competition law regime.

As with Art 101, the Modernisation Regulation (Reg. 1/2003) provided for the transfer of much of the responsibility for enforcement of Art 102 to NCAs. However, as with Art 101, the analysis of the fundamental elements of Art 102 took place before the introduction of the modernisation regulation. Therefore, the decisions are those of the ECJ and CFI. It should be noted that the ECJ and CFI are now known as the Court of Justice and the General Court respectively. However, at the time of the decisions contained within this chapter they were known as the ECJ and CFI.

In deciding whether a breach has occurred, the Commission, NCAs and courts must identify the following:

(a)   The "undertaking/s" which are suspected of being dominant and are accused of abuse of that dominance;

(b)   Whether that undertaking enjoys a dominant position. This is decided firstly by identifying the market within which the undertaking operates and secondly by ascertaining the share of that market controlled by the relevant undertaking/s;

(c)   If the undertaking/s do enjoy a dominant position – are they abusing it?

(d)   Does the abuse affect trade between Member States?

This chapter will examine points 2 and 3.

1   The Market

Before being able to assess whether an undertaking is dominant in a particular market it is necessary to establish what that market is.

To ascertain the market within which an undertaking is operating it is necessary to consider firstly, what is the product an undertaking is selling into the market and secondly, what is the geographical area in which that undertaking sells that product. The Commission and Courts do this by analysing the relevant product market ("RPM") and the relevant geographic market ("RGM"). It may also be necessary to consider how long a particular position in the market is likely to last – this is known as reviewing the relevant temporal market ("RTM").

The cases involving RPM, RGM and RTM demonstrate that the Commission and the accused undertaking will often be locked in a complex battle to define the market in a manner which suits their position. As a result cases can involve very sophisticated economic arguments and often make use of evidence from economic analysts.

1.1 Relevant Product Market

The Commission will usually want to show that the RPM is narrow as this is more likely to result in an undertaking holding a dominant position. Conversely, the accused undertaking will usually want to show that the RPM is wide.

To assist in the analysis of the RPM the Commission and Courts will often look at how likely a consumer of a particular product is to switch to an alternative product and in what circumstances it will do so. This is known as demand side substitutionality, interchangeability or product substitution. If a consumer is likely to switch between particular products easily it is likely that those products form part of the same product market.

The ECJ provided a useful analysis of elements to be taken into account when considering demand side substitutionality in *United Brands Company and United Brands Continentaal BV v Commission* Case 27/76 [1978] 1 CMLR 429 (*"United Brands"*).

United Brands Company and United Brands Continentaal BV v Commission Case 27/76 [1978] 1 CMLR 429

Panel: Kutscher CJ, Sørensen and Bosco PPC, Donner, Mertens de Wilmars, Lord Mackenzie Stuart and Touffait JJ. M. Henri Mayras, Advocate-General

Legislation: Art 102 (ex Art 82)

Facts: United Brands produced bananas and supplied them to a number of distributors in several EU countries. The Commission accused the company of a number of abusive practices. United Brands contested the decision of the Commission in the ECJ. Before reviewing the alleged abusive practices the ECJ reviewed the RPM into which bananas fall. The Commission argued that they formed a distinct market of their own. United Brands argued that they formed part of the wider fresh fruit market.

JUDGMENT

22 For the banana to be regarded as forming a market which is sufficiently differentiated from other fruit markets it must be possible for it to be singled out by such special features distinguishing it from other fruits that it is only to a limited extent interchangeable with them and is only exposed to their competition in a way that is hardly perceptible.

23 The ripening of bananas takes place the whole year round without any season having to be taken into account.

24 Throughout the year production exceeds demand and can satisfy it at any time.

25 Owing to this particular feature the banana is a privileged fruit and its production and marketing can be adapted to the seasonal fluctuations of other fresh fruit which are known and can be computed.

26 There is no unavoidable seasonal substitution since the consumer can obtain this fruit all the year round.

27 Since the banana is a fruit which is always available in sufficient quantities the question whether it can be replaced by other fruits must be determined over the whole of the year for the purpose of ascertaining the degree of competition between it and other fresh fruit.

28 The studies of the banana market on the court's file show that on the latter market there is no significant long term cross-elasticity any more than - as has been mentioned - there is any seasonal substitutability in general between the banana and all the seasonal fruits, as this only exists between the banana and two fruits (peaches and table grapes) in one of the countries (West Germany) of the relevant geographic market.

29 As far as concerns the two fruits available throughout the year (oranges and apples) the first are not interchangeable and in the case of the second there is only a relative degree of substitutability.

30 This small degree of substitutability is accounted for by the specific features of the banana and all the factors which influence consumer choice.

31 The banana has certain characteristics, appearance, taste, softness, seedlessness, easy handling, a constant level of production which enable it to satisfy the constant needs of an important section of the population consisting of the very young, the old and the sick.

32 As far as prices are concerned two FAO studies show that the banana is only affected by the prices - falling prices - of other fruits (and only of peaches and table grapes) during the summer months and mainly in July and then by an amount not exceeding 20%.

33 Although it cannot be denied that during these months and some weeks at the end of the year this product is exposed to competition from other fruits, the flexible way in which the volume of imports and their marketing on the relevant geographic market is adjusted means that the conditions of competition are extremely limited and that its price adapts without any serious difficulties to this situation where supplies of fruit are plentiful.

34 It follows from all these considerations that a very large number of consumers having a constant need for bananas are not noticeably or even appreciably enticed away from the consumption of this product by the arrival of other fresh fruit on the market and that even the personal peak periods only affect it for a limited period of time and to a very limited extent from the point of view of substitutability.

Decipher

The FAO is the Food and Agriculture Organisation of the UN.

Alert

35 Consequently the banana market is a market which is sufficiently distinct from the other fresh fruit markets.

When considering the likelihood of demand side substitution it is also important to consider the test set out in the Commission's Notice on the Definition of the Relevant Market (97/C 372/03) known as the SSNIP test.

In addition to considering how easily consumers will switch between different products, the Commission and Courts will also consider whether another undertaking could easily start offering the product in question. This is known as supply side substitutionality. The ECJ considered this point in the following case.

Nederlandsche Banden – Industrie Michelin NV v Commission (Case 322/81) [1985] 1 CMLR 282

Panel: Mertens de Wilmars CJ, Koopmans , Bahlmann and Galmot PPC, Pescatore, Lord Mackenzie Stuart, O'Keeffe, Due and Everling JJ. Mr. Pieter Verloren Van Themaat Advocate-General

Legislation: Art 102 (ex Art 82)

Facts: Michelin produced tyres for a number of types of vehicles. The Commission found Michelin to be dominant in the market for replacement tyres for lorries, buses and similar vehicles and found that Michelin offered discounts to customers based on arbitrary grounds to tie customers in, rather than on the basis of justifiable grounds such as the quantity of tyres ordered. As part of its appeal Michelin questioned the Commission's assessment of the RPM.

JUDGMENT

37 As the court has repeatedly emphasized, most recently in its judgment of 11 December 1980 in case 31/80 NV L 'Oreal and SA L 'Oreal v PVBA de Nieuwe Amck (1980) ECR 3775, for the purposes of investigating the possibly dominant position of an undertaking on a given market, the possibilities of competition must be judged in the context of the market comprising the totality of the products which, with respect to their characteristics, are particularly suitable for satisfying constant needs and are only to a limited extent interchangeable with other products. However, it must be noted that the determination of the relevant market is useful in assessing whether the undertaking concerned is in a position to prevent effective competition from being maintained and behave to an appreciable extent independently of its competitors and customers and consumers. For this purpose, therefore, an examination limited to the objective characteristics only of the relevant products cannot be sufficient: the competitive conditions and the structure of supply and demand on the market must also be taken into consideration.

38 Moreover, it was for that reason that the Commission and Michelin NV agreed that new, original-equipment tyres should not be taken into consideration in the assessment of market shares. Owing to the particular structure of demand for such tyres characterized by direct orders from car manufacturers, competition in this sphere is in fact governed by completely different factors and rules.

Alert

39 As far as replacement tyres are concerned, the first point which must be made is that at the user level there is no interchangeability between car and van tyres on the one hand and heavy-vehicle tyres on the other. Car and van tyres therefore have no influence at all on competition on the market in heavy-vehicle tyres.

40 Furthermore, the structure of demand for each of those groups of products is different. Most buyers of heavy-vehicle tyres are trade users, particularly haulage undertakings, for whom, as the Commission explained, the purchase of replacement tyres represents an item of considerable expenditure and who constantly ask their tyre dealers for advice and long-term specialized services adapted to their specific needs. On the other hand, for the average buyer of car or van tyres the purchase of tyres is an occasional event and even if the buyer operates a business he does not expect such specialized advice and service adapted to specific needs. Hence the sale of heavy-vehicle tyres requires a particularly specialized distribution network which is not the case with the distribution of car and van tyres.

41 The final point which must be made is that there is no elasticity of supply between tyres for heavy vehicles and car tyres owing to significant differences in production techniques and in the plant and tools needed for their manufacture. The fact that time and considerable investment are required in order to modify production plant for the manufacture of light-vehicle tyres instead of heavy-vehicle tyres or vice versa means that there is no discernible relationship between the two categories of tyre enabling production to be adapted to demand on the market. Moreover, that was why in 1977, when the supply of tyres for heavy vehicles was insufficient, Michelin NV decided to grant an extra bonus instead of using surplus production capacity for car tyres to meet demand.

42 The Commission rightly examined the structure of the market and demand primarily at the level of dealers to whom Michelin NV applied the practice in question. Michelin NV has itself stated, although in another context, that it was compelled to change its discount system to take account of the tendency towards specialization amongst its dealers, some of whom, such as garage owners, no longer sold tyres for heavy vehicles and vans. This confirms the differences existing in the structure of demand between different groups of dealers. Nor has Michelin NV disputed that the distinction drawn between tyres for heavy vehicles, vans and cars is also applied by all its competitors, especially as regards discount terms, even if in the case of certain types of tyre the distinctions drawn by different manufacturers may vary in detail.

43 Nevertheless, it cannot be deduced from the fact that the conduct to which exception is taken in this case affects dealers that Michelin NV's position ought to be assessed on the basis of the proportion of Michelin heavy-vehicle tyres in the dealers' total turnover. Since it is a question of investigating whether Michelin NV holds a dominant position in the case of certain products, it is unimportant that the dealers also deal in other products if there is no competition between those products and the products in question.

44 On the other hand, in deciding whether a dominant position exists, neither the absence of elasticity of supply between different types and dimensions of tyres for

heavy vehicles, which is due to differences in the conditions of production, nor the absence of interchangeability and elasticity of demand between those types and dimensions of tyre from the point of view of the specific needs of the user allow a number of smaller markets, reflecting those types and dimensions, to be distinguished, as Michelin NV suggests. Those differences between different types and dimensions of tyre are not vitally important for dealers, who must meet demand from customers for the whole range of heavy-vehicle tyres. Furthermore, in the absence of any specialization on the part of the undertakings concerned, such differences in the type and dimensions of a product are not a crucial factor in the assessment of an undertaking's market position because in view of their similarity and the manner in which they complement one another at the technical level, the conditions of competition on the market are the same for all the types and dimensions of the product.

45 In establishing that Michelin NV has a dominant position the Commission was therefore right to assess its market share with reference to replacement tyres for lorries, buses and similar vehicles and to exclude consideration of car and van tyres.

1.2 Relevant Geographic Market

Once the RPM has been determined it is necessary to establish that the potential abuse is "...within the common market or in a substantial part of it...". To do this the Commission must determine the RGM. The ECJ defined the RGM in *United Brands*.

United Brands Company and United Brands Continentaal BV v Commission Case 27/76 [1978] 1 CMLR 429

Facts: Having decided the RPM as discussed above the ECJ moved on to discuss the RGM.

JUDGMENT

43 The applicant draws the conclusion from all these findings that the geographic market taken by the Commission includes areas in which the conditions of competition are so different that they cannot be considered as constituting a single market.

44 The conditions for the application of Article 82 to an undertaking in a dominant position presuppose the clear delimitation of the substantial part of the common market in which it may be able to engage in abuses which hinder effective competition and this is an area where the objective conditions of competition applying to the product in question must be the same for all traders.

 Alert

45 The community has not established a common organization of the agricultural market in bananas.

46 Consequently import arrangements vary considerably from one member state to another and reflect a specific commercial policy peculiar to the states concerned.

47 This explains why for example the French market owing to its national organization is restricted upstream by a particular import arrangement and obstructed downstream by a retail price monitored by the administration.

48 This market, in addition to adopting certain measures relating to a "target price" ("prix objectif") fixed each year and to packaging and grading standards and the minimum qualities required, reserves about two thirds of the market for the production of the overseas departments and one third to that of certain countries enjoying preferential relations with France (ivory coast, Madagascar, Cameroon) the bananas whereof are imported duty- free, and it includes a system the running of which is entrusted to the "comite interprofessionnel bananier" ("C.I.B.").

49 The united kingdom market enjoys "commonwealth preferences", a system of which the main feature is the maintenance of a level of production favouring the developing countries of the commonwealth and of a price paid to the associations of producers directly linked to the selling price of the green banana charged in the united kingdom.

50 On the Italian market, since the abolition in 1965 of the state monopoly responsible for marketing bananas, a national system of quota restrictions has been introduced, the ministry for shipping and the exchange control office supervising the imports and the charter parties relating to the foreign ships which carry the bananas.

51 The effect of the national organization of these three markets is that the applicant's bananas do not compete on equal terms with the other bananas sold in these states which benefit from a preferential system and the Commission was right to exclude these three national markets from the geographic market under consideration.

 Alert

52 On the other hand the six other states are markets which are completely free, although the applicable tariff provisions and transport costs are of necessity different but not discriminatory, and in which the conditions of competition are the same for all.

53 From the standpoint of being able to engage in free competition these six states form an area which is sufficiently homogeneous to be considered in its entirety.

54 UBC has arranged for its subsidiary in Rotterdam - UBCBV - to market its products. UBCBV is for this purpose a single centre for the whole of this part of the community.

55 Transport costs do not in fact stand in the way of the distribution policy chosen by UBC which consists in selling F.O.R. Rotterdam and Bremerhaven, the two ports where the bananas are unloaded.

56 These are factors which go to make relevant market a single market.

57 It follows from all these considerations that the geographic market as determined by the Commission which constitutes a substantial part of the common market must be regarded as the relevant market for the purpose of determining whether the applicant may be in a dominant position.

1.3 Relevant Temporal Market

Although not as fundamental as the RPM and RGM in establishing the relevant market, regard should be had as to the RTM. Essentially this involves an analysis as to whether dominance in a particular market is likely to be short-lived because other undertakings are able to easily produce rival products.

Europemballage Corporation and Continental Can Company Inc. v Commission of the European Communities Case 6-72 [1976] 1 CMLR 587

Panel: Mertens de Wilmars CJ, Monaco and O'Keeffe JJ. Herr Gerhard Reischl, Advocate-General

Legislation: Art 102 (ex Art 82)

Facts: Continental Can manufactured metal packages and packaging materials of paper and plastic, and machines for manufacturing and using those packaging materials. The Commission found that Continental Can, through a subsidiary, occupied a dominant position in this market and questioned the validity of a corporate transaction entered into on the basis that it may breach competition law.

JUDGMENT

33 In this context recitals nos. 5 to 7 of the second part of the decision deal in turn with a " market for light containers for canned meat products ", a " market for light containers for canned seafood ", and a " market for metal closures for the food packing industry, other than crown corks ", all allegedly dominated by SLW and in which the disputed merger threatens to eliminate competition. The decision does not, however, give any details of how these three markets differ from each other, and must therefore be considered separately. Similarly, nothing is said about how these three markets differ from the general market for light metal containers, namely the market for metal containers for fruit and vegetables, condensed milk, olive oil, fruit juices and chemico-technical products. In order to be regarded as constituting a distinct market, the products in question must be individualized, not only by the mere fact that they are used for packing certain products, but by particular characteristics of production which make them specifically suitable for this purpose. Consequently, a dominant position on the market for light metal containers for meat and fish cannot be decisive, as long as it has not been proved that competitors from other sectors of the market for light metal containers are not in a position to enter this market, by a simple adaptation, with sufficient strength to create a serious counterweight.

1.4 Establishing Dominance

The ECJ defined dominance in *United Brands* as follows:

63 Article 82 is an application of the general objective of the activities of the community laid down by article 3(f) of the treaty: the institution of a system ensuring that competition in the common market is not distorted.

64 This article prohibits any abuse by an undertaking of a dominant position in a substantial part of the common market in so far as it may affect trade between member states.

65 The dominant position referred to in this article relates to a position of economic strength enjoyed by an undertaking which enables it to prevent effective competition being maintained on the relevant market by giving it the power to behave to an

appreciable extent independently of its competitors, customers and ultimately of its consumers.

66 In general a dominant position derives from a combination of several factors which, taken separately, are not necessarily determinative.

67 In order to find out whether UBC is an undertaking in a dominant position on the relevant market it is necessary first of all to examine its structure and then the situation on the said market as far as competition is concerned.

68 In doing so it may be advisable to take account if need be of the facts put forward as acts amounting to abuses without necessarily having to acknowledge that they are abuses.

The ECJ subsequently added to this definition in the following case.

Hoffman-La-Roche & Co v Commission **Case 85/76 [1979] 3 CMLR 211**

Panel: Kutscher CJ; Mertens de Wilmars and Lord Mackenzie Stuart PPC; Donner, Pescatore, Sørensen, O'Keeffe, Bosco and Touffait JJ. Herr Gerhard Reischl, Advocate-General

Legislation: Art 102 (ex Art 82)

Facts: Hoffmann-La-Roche produced vitamins. The Commission found that Hoffman-La-Roche held a dominant position in the markets for certain vitamins and accused the company of abusing that position by entering into exclusive agreements or agreements which provided discounts on arbitrary grounds rather than justifiable grounds such as the quantity of goods ordered.

JUDGMENT

38 Art 82 is an application of the general objective of the activities of the community laid down by article 3 (f) of the treaty namely, the institution of a system ensuring that competition in the common market is not distorted.

Art 82 prohibits any abuse by an undertaking of a dominant position in a substantial part of the common market in so far as it may affect trade between member states.

The dominant position thus referred to relates to a position of economic strength enjoyed by an undertaking which enables it to prevent effective competition being maintained on the relevant market by affording it the power to behave to an appreciable extent independently of its competitors, its customers and ultimately of the consumers.

 Alert

39 Such a position does not preclude some competition, which it does where there is a monopoly or a quasi-monopoly, but enables the undertaking which profits by it, if not to determine, at least to have an appreciable influence on the conditions under which that competition will develop, and in any case to act largely in disregard of it so long as such conduct does not operate to its detriment.

A dominant position must also be distinguished from parallel courses of conduct which are peculiar to oligopolies in that in an oligopoly the courses of conduct interact, while in the case of an undertaking occupying a dominant position the conduct of the undertaking which derives profits from that position is to a great extent determined unilaterally.

The existence of a dominant position may derive from several factors which, taken separately, are not necessarily determinative but among these factors a highly important one is the existence of very large market shares.

40 A substantial market share as evidence of the existence of a dominant position is not a constant factor and its importance varies from market to market according to the structure of these markets, especially as far as production, supply and demand are concerned.

Even though each group of vitamins constitutes a separate market, these different markets, as has emerged from the examination of their structure, nevertheless have a sufficient number of features in common to make it possible for the same criteria to be applied to them as far as concerns the importance of the market shares for the purpose of determining whether there is a dominant position or not.

41 Furthermore although the importance of the market shares may vary from one market to another the view may legitimately be taken that very large shares are in themselves, and save in exceptional circumstances, evidence of the existence of a dominant position.

An undertaking which has a very large market share and holds it for some time, by means of the volume of production and the scale of the supply which it stands for - without those having much smaller market shares being able to meet rapidly the demand from those who would like to break away from the undertaking which has the largest market share - is by virtue of that share in a position of strength which makes it an unavoidable trading partner and which, already because of this secures for it, at the very least during relatively long periods, that freedom of action which is the special feature of a dominant position.

Dominance is often evident therefore either from the substantial market share of an undertaking or from the barriers to entry into that market faced by potential competitors.

2 Abuse of Dominance

Dominant undertakings are deemed to have a special responsibility not to distort genuine competition. The ECJ emphasised this in *Michelin:*

57 It is not possible to uphold the objections made against those arguments by Michelin NV, supported on this point by the French government, that Michelin NV is thus penalized for the quality of its products and services. A finding that an undertaking has a dominant position is not in itself a recrimination but simply means that, irrespective of the reasons for which it has such a dominant position, the undertaking concerned has a special responsibility not to allow its conduct to impair genuine undistorted competition on the common market.

Art 102 (ex Art 82) itself provides a starting point. You should refer to Art 102 when reading the rest of this Chapter.

The ECJ has found particular types of behaviour to constitute abuse.

2.1 Refusal to Supply

United Brands Company and United Brands Continentaal BV v Commission Case 27/76 [1978] CMLR

Facts: see earlier.

JUDGMENT

151 The court's examination must be limited to the clause relating to the prohibition of the resale of green bananas in the form in which it was notified to the Commission on 15 November 1968 without it being necessary to consider the clause as drawn up by UBC on 31 January 1976, that is to say at a date subsequent to the Commission's decision.

152 The clause applied in Belgium, Denmark and the Netherlands, in so far as it has been drawn up in writing, prohibited the resale of bananas while still green whether branded or unbranded and even between ripeners of chiquita bananas.

153 Since UBC thought it should state in the circular letter of 31 January 1976, which it sent to all ripener/distributors including those established in Germany, that the clause had not been put in writing for Germany, it thereby impliedly acknowledges that the said clause was in force on the German market, since it had clearly been implied or mentioned orally.

154 Under the terms of the clause UBC required their customers to ensure forthwith that the bananas in their possession are not resold to foreign dealers; it had imposed the same requirement on its foreign customers as far as the Netherlands are concerned. It would not hesitate to take such steps as it deems to be necessary if the foregoing is not complied with in some way or other '.

155 This wording implies that UBC, far from rejecting the idea of imposing sanctions on duly appointed ripener/distributors which do not comply with its directions, held out this possibility as a threat.

156 Moreover Olesen unquestionably experienced the harsh effects of this clause after UBC refused to supply it and it wanted to obtain supplies of chiquita bananas from Scipio and the duly appointed Danish distributors.

157 To impose on the ripener the obligation not to resell bananas so long as he has not had them ripened and to cut down the operations of such a ripener to contacts only with retailers is a restriction of competition.

158 Although it is commendable and lawful to pursue a policy of quality, especially by choosing sellers according to objective criteria relating to the qualifications of the

seller, his staff and his facilities, such a practice can only be justified if it does not raise obstacles, the effect of which goes beyond the objective to be attained.

159 In this case, although these conditions for selection have been laid down in a way which is objective and not discriminatory, the prohibition on resale imposed upon duly appointed chiquita ripeners and the prohibition of the resale of unbranded bananas - even if the perishable nature of the banana in practice restricted the opportunities of reselling to the duration of a specific period of time - when without any doubt an abuse of the dominant position since they limit markets to the prejudice of consumers and affects trade between member states, in particular by partitioning national markets.

 Alert

160 Thus UBC's organization of the market confined the ripeners to the role of suppliers of the local market and prevented them from developing their capacity to trade vis-à-vis UBC, which moreover tightened its economic hold on them by supplying less goods than they ordered.

161 It follows from all these considerations that the clause at issue forbidding the sale of green bananas infringes Art 82 of the treaty.

162 On this point the contested decision is therefore justified.

Microsoft v Commission Case T-201/04 R [2005] 4 CMLR 5

Panel: Vesterdorf P, Jaeger, Pirrung, García-Valdecasas, Tiili, Azizi, Cooke, A.W.H. Meij, Norwood, Martins Ribeiro, Wiszniewska-Białecka, Vadapalas and Labucka, JJ

Legislation: Art 102 (ex Art 82)

Facts: In this case the CFI reviewed the Decision of the Commission in relation to refusal to supply interoperability information and also abuse of dominance in the market for media players. The CFI went on to uphold the decision of the Commission in respect of all but one element, which is not relevant to matters set out below. The summary of the CFI provides a useful overview of the potential abuse caused by refusal to supply and "tying", increasingly relevant matters with the growth of digital technology where one undertaking may need to make its software "plug in" to the software or hardware of a competitor.

JUDGMENT

III Abuse of a dominant position

A – Refusal to supply and authorise the use of interoperability information

36   The first abusive conduct in which Microsoft is found to have engaged consists in its refusal to supply its competitors with 'interoperability information' and to authorise the use of that information for the purpose of developing and distributing products competing with Microsoft's own products on the work group server operating systems market, between October 1998 and the date of notification of the contested decision (Article 2(a) of the contested decision). That conduct is described at recitals 546 to 791 to the contested decision.

37   For the purposes of the contested decision, 'interoperability information' is the 'complete and accurate specifications for all the protocols [implemented] in Windows work group server operating systems and ... used by Windows work group servers to deliver file and print services and group and user administrative services, including the Windows domain controller services, Active Directory services and "group Policy" services to Windows work group networks' (Article 1(1) of the contested decision).

38   'Windows work group network' is defined as 'any group of Windows client PCs and Windows work group servers linked together via a computer network' (Article 1(7) of the contested decision).

39   A 'protocol' is defined as 'a set of rules of interconnection and interaction between various instances of Windows work group server operating systems and Windows client PC operating systems running on different computers in a Windows work group network' (Article 1(2) of the contested decision).

40   In the contested decision, the Commission emphasises that the refusal in question does not relate to Microsoft's 'source code', but only to specifications of the protocols concerned, that is to say, to a detailed description of what the software in question must achieve, in contrast to the implementations, consisting in the implementation of the code on the computer (recitals 24 and 569 to the contested decision). It states, in particular, that it 'does not contemplate ordering Microsoft to allow copying of Windows by third parties' (recital 572 to the contested decision).

41   The Commission further considers that Microsoft's refusal to Sun is part of a general pattern of conduct (recitals 573 to 577 to the contested decision). It also asserts that Microsoft's conduct involves a disruption of previous, higher levels of supply (recitals 578 to 584 to the contested decision), causes a risk of elimination of competition on the work group server operating systems (recitals 585 to 692 to the contested decision) and has a negative effect on technical development and on consumer welfare (recitals 693 to 708 to the contested decision).

42   Last, the Commission rejects Microsoft's arguments that its refusal is objectively justified (recitals 709 to 778 to the contested decision)

B – Tying of the Windows client PC operating system and Windows Media Player

43   The second abusive conduct in which Microsoft is found to have engaged consists in the fact that from May 1999 to the date of notification of the contested decision Microsoft made the availability of the Windows client PC operating system conditional on the simultaneous acquisition of the Windows Media Player software (Article 2(b) of the contested decision). That conduct is described at recitals 792 to 989 to the contested decision.

44   In the contested decision, the Commission considers that that conduct satisfies the conditions for a finding of a tying abuse for the purposes of Art 82 EC (recitals 794 to 954 to the contested decision). First, it reiterates that Microsoft has a dominant position on the client PC operating systems market (recital 799 to the contested decision). Second, it considers that streaming media players and client PC operating systems constitute separate products (recitals 800 to 825 to the contested decision).

Third, it asserts that Microsoft does not give consumers the opportunity to buy Windows without Windows Media Player (recitals 826 to 834 to the contested decision). Fourth, it contends that the tying in question restricts competition on the media players market (recitals 835 to 954 to the contested decision).

45   Last, the Commission rejects Microsoft's arguments to the effect that, first, the tying in question produces efficiency gains capable of offsetting the anti-competitive effects identified in the contested decision (recitals 955 to 970 to the contested decision) and, second, Microsoft had no interest in 'anti-competitive' tying (recitals 971 to 977 to the contested decision).

Later in the decision the CFI reviewed the approach of the Commission in its interpretation of Art 102 (ex Art 82):

228   In the second place, the Court observes that the Commission assessed the degree of interoperability by reference to what, in its view, was necessary in order to enable developers of non-Microsoft work group server operating systems to remain viably on the market (see, in particular, footnote 712 and recital 779 to the contested decision).

229   The correctness of that approach is not open to dispute. Art.82 EC deals with the conduct of one or more economic operators involving the abuse of a position of economic strength which enables the operator concerned to hinder the maintenance of effective competition on the relevant market by allowing it to behave to an appreciable extent independently of its competitors, its customers and, ultimately, consumers (Joined Cases C-359/96 P and C-396/96 P *Compagnie maritime belge transports and Others* v *Commission* [2000] ECR I-1365, paragraph 34). Furthermore, whilst the finding of a dominant position does not in itself imply any criticism of the undertaking concerned, that undertaking has a special responsibility, irrespective of the causes of that position, not to allow its conduct to impair genuine undistorted competition on the common market (Case 322/81 *Michelin* v *Commission* [1983] ECR 3461, paragraph 57, and Case T-228/97 *Irish Sugar* v *Commission* [1999] ECR II-2969, paragraph 112). Should it be established in the present case that the existing degree of interoperability does not enable developers of non-Microsoft work group server operating systems to remain viably on the market for those operating systems, it follows that the maintenance of effective competition on that market is being hindered

2.2 Directly or Indirectly Imposing Unfair Prices

Hoffman-La-Roche & Co v Commission Case 85/76 [1979] 3 CMLR 211

Facts: Having found Hoffman-La Roche to be dominant in the relevant market the ECJ considered whether the company had abused that dominance through exclusivity agreements and fidelity rebates.

JUDGMENT

80 According to the contested decision the applicant has abused its dominant position by concluding with 22 large purchasers of vitamins contracts of sale - about 30 (some of them moreover were renewals with or without amendments of a previous contract) - under which these purchasers undertook to obtain all or most of their requirements of vitamins or certain vitamins expressly mentioned therein exclusively from Roche or which gave them an incentive to do so by including a promise of a discount which the Commission classifies as a fidelity rebate.

According to the Commission (recitals 22 to 24 of the contested decision) the exclusivity agreements and the fidelity rebates complained of are an abuse within the meaning of Art. 86 of the treaty, on the one hand, because they distort competition between producers by depriving customers of the undertaking in a dominant position of the opportunity to choose their sources of supply and, on the other hand, because their effect was to apply dissimilar conditions to equivalent transactions with other trading partners, thereby placing them at a competitive disadvantage, in that Roche offers two purchasers two different prices for an identical quantity of the same product depending on whether these two buyers agree or not to forego obtaining their supplies from Roche's competitors.

81 The contracts at issue are for the sale of vitamins which belong to one or more of the groups in respect of which a dominant position has been found to exist to purchasers owning within the common market undertakings for which part or all of these vitamins are intended.

...

89 An undertaking which is in a dominant position on a market and ties purchasers - even if it does so at their request - by an obligation or promise on their part to obtain all or most of their requirements exclusively from the said undertaking abuses its dominant position within the meaning of article 86 of the treaty, whether the obligation in question is stipulated without further qualification or whether it is undertaken in consideration of the grant of a rebate.

The same applies if the said undertaking, without tying the purchasers by a formal obligation, applies, either under the terms of agreements concluded with these purchasers or unilaterally, a system of fidelity rebates, that is to say discounts conditional on the customer's obtaining all or most of its requirements - whether the quantity of its purchases be large or small - from the undertaking in a dominant position.

90 Obligations of this kind to obtain supplies exclusively from a particular undertaking, whether or not they are in consideration of rebates or of the granting of fidelity rebates intended to give the purchaser an incentive to obtain his supplies exclusively from the undertaking in a dominant position, are incompatible with the objective of undistorted competition within the common market, because - unless there are exceptional circumstances which may make an agreement between undertakings in the context of article 81 and in particular of paragraph (3) of that article, permissible - they are not

 Alert

based on an economic transaction which justifies this burden or benefit but are designed to deprive the purchaser of or restrict his possible choices of sources of supply and to deny other producers access to the market.

The fidelity rebate, unlike quantity rebates exclusively linked with the volume of purchases from the producer concerned, is designed through the grant of a financial advantage to prevent customers from obtaining their supplies from competing producers.

Furthermore the effect of fidelity rebates is to apply dissimilar conditions to equivalent transactions with other trading parties in that two purchasers pay a different price for the same quantity of the same product depending on whether they obtain their supplies exclusively from the undertaking in a dominant position or have several sources of supply.

Finally these practices by an undertaking in a dominant position and especially on an expanding market tend to consolidate this position by means of a form of competition which is not based on the transactions effected and is therefore distorted.

The ECJ then went on to consider specific clauses in contracts with customers, which Hoffman-La-Roche sought to argue allowed for rebates based on the quantity of purchases – which could be permissible. The Commission argued that the rebates were disguised fidelity rebates.

98 Although the contracts at issue contain elements which appear at first sight to be of a quantitative nature as far as concerns their connexion with the granting of a rebate on aggregate purchases, an examination of them however shows that they are in fact a specially worked out form of fidelity rebate.

99 In the first place it is noticeable that this particular form of rebate is incorporated in those very contracts in which the undertaking by the purchaser to obtain supplies was drawn up in the form which placed him under the least constraint, namely that the purchaser was to obtain 'most of his requirements', so that the purchaser concerned was left with considerable freedom of action.

The indeterminate nature of the undertaking thus worded is to a great extent offset by an estimate of annual requirements and by the granting of a rebate increasing in accordance with the percentage of the requirements which are met and this progressive rate is clearly a powerful incentive to obtain the maximum percentage of the said requirements from Roche.

100 This method of calculating the rebates differs from the granting of quantitative rebates, linked solely to the volume of purchases from the producers concerned in that the rebates at issue are not dependent on quantities fixed objectively and applicable to all possible purchasers but on estimates made, from case to case, for each customer according to the latter's presumed capacity of absorption, the objective which it is sought to attain being not the maximum quantity but the maximum requirements.

101 Consequently the Commission was also right to regard the said contracts containing fidelity rebates as an abuse of a dominant position.

Alert

2.3 May Affect Inter-state Trade

All that is required is to show that the behaviour might affect interstate trade – the test is the same as for Art 101 (ex Art 81).

Further Reading

Fuller, Baden: 'Economic Analysis of the Existence of a Dominant Position' [1979] 4 ELR 423

Turnbull, S: 'Barriers to Entry, Article 86 EC and the Abuse of a Dominant Position: An Economic Critique of European Community Competition Law' [1996] ECLR 96

5

Free Movement of Goods

Chris Garside

Introduction

One of the fundamental aims of the EU is to lay the foundation for the free movement of goods between Member States. It is one of the four cornerstone freedoms, the others being the free movement of persons (see Chapter 8), services (see Chapter 7) and capital. These freedoms are necessary to bring about a genuine common market.

Member States can resist this freedom by attempting to protect those producing goods within their territory from goods imported from other Member States. This protectionism can take a number of forms from outright and obvious prohibitions or extra charges on those goods to more subtle forms of restriction. A number of Articles deal with each of these forms of protectionism.

These are Art 30 (ex Art 25), Art 110 (ex Art 90), EC Art 34 (ex Art 28), Art 25 (ex Art 29) and Art 36 (ex Art 30 EC). You should familiarise yourself with them.

1 Preliminary Issues

1.1 Definition of Goods

Commission v Italy Case 7/68 [1969] CMLR 1 (the "Italian Glass" case)

Panel: Lecourt P, A. Trabucchi, Mertens de Wilmars, Donner, Strauss, Monaco and Pescatore JJ. M. Joseph Gand, Advocate-General

Legislation: Art 30 (ex Art 25)

Facts: The Italian government imposed a charge on artistic works and argued that such works do not come within the definition of goods. The ECJ reviewed the definition of "goods".

JUDGMENT

Under Art 9 of the Treaty the community is based on a customs union ' which shall cover all trade in goods '. By goods, within the meaning of that provision, there must be understood products which can be valued in money and which are capable, as such, of forming the subject of commercial transactions.

2 Fiscal Barriers: Customs Duties and Charges Having Equivalent Effect: Art 30

Customs duties between Member States have been prohibited since the formation of the common market. The result is that goods should be free to move within the common market without being subject to such duties, even if the purpose of the duty is stated to be something other than protectionism, as in the *Italian Glass* case where the purpose stated was the retention of art. It is the effect which is the important factor.

The more subtle forms of border based levy are "charges having equivalent effect" (CEE). The most comprehensive case which provides a clear idea as to the nature of a CEE is *Commission v Italy* (the *"Statistical Levy"* case) Case 24/68 [1971] CMLR 611.

Commission v Italy Case 24/68 (the *"Statistical Levy"* case) [1971] CMLR 611

Panel: Lecourt P, Trabucchi, Mertens de Wilmars, Donner, Strauss, Monaco and Pescatore JJ. Herr Karl Roemer, Advocate-General

Legislation: Art 30 (ex Art 25)

Facts: The Italian government imposed a small levy on goods exported to other Member States claiming that the levy was imposed for the purpose of collecting statistical data for use in the analysis of trade patterns.

> JUDGMENT
>
> 7 It follows from the system as a whole and from the general and absolute nature of the prohibition of any customs duty applicable to goods moving between Member States that customs duties are prohibited independently of any consideration of the purpose for which they were introduced and the destination of the revenue obtained therefrom.
>
> The justification for this prohibition is based on the fact that any pecuniary charge, however small, imposed on goods by reason of the fact that they cross a frontier constitutes an obstacle to the movement of such goods.
>
> 8 The extension of the prohibition of customs duties to charges having equivalent effect is intended to supplement the prohibition against obstacles to trade created by such duties by increasing its efficiency.
>
> The use of these two complementary concepts thus tends, in trade between Member States, to avoid the imposition of any pecuniary charge on goods circulating within the community by virtue of the fact that they cross a national frontier.
>
> 9 Thus, in order to ascribe to a charge an effect equivalent to a customs duty, it is important to consider this effect in the light of the objectives of the Treaty, in the parts, titles and chapters in which Arts. 9, 12, 13 and 16 are to be found, particularly in relation to the free movement of goods.
>
> Consequently, any pecuniary charge, however small and whatever its designation and mode of application, which is imposed unilaterally on domestic or foreign goods by reason of the fact that they cross a frontier, and which is not a customs duty in the strict sense, constitutes a charge having equivalent effect within the meaning of Arts 9, 12, 13 and 16 of the Treaty, even if it is not imposed for the benefit of the state, is not discriminatory or protective in effect and if the product on which the charge is imposed is not in competition with any domestic product.
>
> 10 It follows from all the provisions referred to and from their relationship with the other provisions of the Treaty that the prohibition of new customs duties or charges having equivalent effect, linked to the principle of the free movement of goods, constitutes a fundamental rule which, without prejudice to the other provisions of the Treaty, does not permit of any exceptions.

 Alert

2.1 Charges That Do Not Constitute a Customs Duty or a Charge Having Equivalent Effect

Although there are no defences to Art 30 the ECJ has recognised three circumstances where a charge on imports will not constitute a customs duty or a CEE and they were discussed in the case of *Commission v Germany* Case 18/87 [1990] 1 CMLR 561.

Commission v Germany Case 18/87 [1990] 1 CMLR 561

Panel: Lord Mackenzie Stuart CJ, Due, Moitinho de Almeida and Rodriguez Iglesias PPC, Koopmans, Everling, Galmot, Kakouris and O'Higgins JJ. Sig. Federico Mancini, Advocate-General

Legislation: Art 30 (ex Art 25)

Facts: The German government charged a fee to cover the costs of veterinary inspections on imported live animals. The inspections were required under a Directive regulating the protection of animals during international transport. The ECJ discussed whether the inspection fee was a CEE and laid down four requirements for when an inspection fee would not constitute a CEE.

JUDGMENT

5 It should be observed in the first place that, as the Court has held on a number of occasions, the justification for the prohibition of customs duties and any charges having an equivalent effect lies in the fact that any pecuniary charge, however small, imposed on goods by reason of the fact that they cross a frontier, constitutes an obstacle to the movement of goods which is aggravated by the resulting administrative formalities. It follows that any pecuniary charge, whatever its designation and mode of application, which is imposed unilaterally on goods by reason of the fact that they cross a frontier and is not a customs duty in the strict sense constitutes a charge having an equivalent effect to a customs duty within the meaning of Articles 9, 12, 13 and 16 of the Treaty.

6 However, the Court has held that such a charge escapes that classification if it relates to a general system of internal dues applied systematically and in accordance with the same criteria to domestic products and imported products alike (judgment of 31 May 1979 in Case 132/78 Denkavit v France ((1979)) ECR 1923), if it constitutes payment for a service in fact rendered to the economic operator of a sum in proportion to the service (judgment of 9 November 1983 in Case 158/82 Commission v Denmark ((1983)) ECR 3573), or again, subject to certain conditions, if it attaches to inspections carried out to fulfil obligations imposed by Community law (judgment of 25 January 1977 in Case 46/76 Bauhuis v Netherlands ((1977)) ECR 5).

 Alert

7 The contested fee, which is payable on importation and transit, cannot be regarded as relating to a general system of internal dues. Nor does it constitute payment for a service rendered to the operator, because this condition is satisfied only if the operator in question obtains a definite specific benefit (see judgment of 1 July 1969 in Case 24/68 *Commission v Italy* ((1969)) ECR 193), which is not the case if the inspection serves to guarantee, in the public interest, the health and life of animals in international

transport (see judgment of 20 March 1984 in Case 314/82 *Commission v Belgium* ((1984)) ECR 1543).

8 Since the contested fee was charged in connection with inspections carried out pursuant to a Community provision, it should be noted that according to the case-law of the Court (judgment of 25 January 1977 in *Bauhuis*, cited above; judgment of 12 July 1977 *Commission v Netherlands* ((1977)) ECR 1355; judgment of 31 January 1984 in Case 1/83 *IFG v Freistaat Bayern* ((1984)) ECR 349) such fees may not be classified as charges having an effect equivalent to a customs duty if the following conditions are satisfied :

(a)   they do not exceed the actual costs of the inspections in connection with which they are charged;

(b)   the inspections in question are obligatory and uniform for all the products concerned in the Community;

(c)   they are prescribed by Community law in the general interest of the Community;

(d)   they promote the free movement of goods, in particular by neutralizing obstacles which could arise from unilateral measures of inspection adopted in accordance with Article 36 of the Treaty.

9 In this instance these conditions are satisfied by the contested fee.

Alert

Conceria Daniele Bresciani v Amministrazione delle Finanz Case 87/75 [1976] 2 CMLR 62

Panel: R. Lecourt P; Judges H. Kutscher, A. M. Donner, J. Mertens de Wilmars, M. Sørensen, Lord Mackenzie Stuart and A. O'Keeffe JJ. Sig. Alberto Trabucchi, Advocate-General

Legislation: Art 30 (ex Art 25)

Facts: The Italian government imposed a charge relating to compulsory inspections on imported raw cowhides on the basis that such inspections were justified for veterinary and public health reasons. The ECJ considered whether a charge could be justified if a similar charge applied to goods produced in the Member State:

11 The fact that the domestic production is, through other charges, subjected to a similar burden matters little unless those charges and the duty in question are applied according to the same criteria and at the same stage of production, thus making it possible for them to be regarded as falling within a general system of internal taxation applying systematically and in the same way to domestic and imported products.

2.2 Discriminatory Internal Taxation: Art 110

It is sometimes difficult to distinguish between a CEE and an internal tax. The ECJ discussed this point in the following case.

Commission v France (the "Reprographic Machinery" case) Case 90/79 [1981] 3 CMLR 1

Panel: Mertens de Wilmars CJ; Pescatore, Lord Mackenzie Stuart and Koopmans PPC; O'Keeffe, Touffait and Due JJ. Mr. Jean-Pierre Warner, Advocate-General

Legislation: Art 110 (ex Art 90)

Facts: The French government introduced a levy on the use of reprographic machinery charged at the rate of 3% on sales, otherwise than for export, and a similar tax on imports of such machines.

JUDGMENT

12 Well-established case-law of the court is to the effect that the prohibition laid down by Arts 9, 12 and 13 of the Treaty in regard to charges having equivalent effect covers any charge exacted at the time of or on account of importation which, being borne specifically by an imported product to the exclusion of the similar domestic product, has the result of altering the cost price of the imported product thereby producing the same restrictive effect on the free movement of goods as a customs duty.

13 The essential feature of a charge having an effect equivalent to a customs duty which distinguishes it from an internal tax therefore resides in the fact that the former is borne solely by an imported product as such whilst the latter is borne both by imported and domestic products.

14 The court has however recognized that even a charge which is borne by a product imported from another member state, when there is no identical or similar domestic product, does not constitute a charge having equivalent effect but internal taxation within the meaning of Art 95 of the Treaty if it relates to a general system of internal dues applied systematically to categories of products in accordance with objective criteria irrespective of the origin of the products.

15 Those considerations demonstrate that even if it were necessary in some cases, for the purpose of classifying a charge borne by imported products, to equate extremely low domestic production with its non-existence, that would not mean that the levy in question would necessarily have to be regarded as a charge having an effect equivalent to a customs duty. In particular, that will not be so if the levy is part of a general system on internal dues applying systematically to categories of products according to the criteria indicated above.

 Alert

16 The court is of the opinion that the particular features of the levy in issue lead to its being accepted as forming part of such a general system of internal dues. That follows first from its inclusion in taxation arrangements which have their origin in the breach made in legal systems for the protection of copyright by the increase in the use of reprography and which are designed to subject, if only indirectly, the users of those processes to a charge which compensates for that which they would normally have to bear.

2.3 Similar Goods

When investigating whether there has been discrimination against particular imported goods under Art 110, the courts must review firstly whether the comparison product within the member state is genuinely similar. If it is then the courts will consider whether the discrimination is the more obvious direct discrimination or more subtle indirect discrimination. If the goods are non-similar the analysis is carried out under Art 110(2), which is considered further below.

2.4 Direct and Indirect Forms of Discrimination

Direct discrimination is easily identifiable, as the tax system will openly treat imported goods less favourably than similar domestic goods. Indirect discrimination is harder to identify, as it will not on the face of it appear to be discriminatory but will in some way twist the situation in favour of the goods produced within that Member State. One of the best examples is the case of *Humblot v Directeur des Services Fiscaux* Case 112/84 [1986] 2 CMLR 338.

Humblot v Directeur des Services Fiscaux **Case 112/84 [1986] 2 CMLR 338**

Panel: Bosco PC, Pescatore, Koopmans, Everling, Bahlmann, Galmot and Joliet JJ. Mr. Pieter Verloren Van Themaat Advocate-General

Legislation: Art 110 (ex Art 90)

Facts: Humblot paid significant tax on a car with an engine size of 36CV. The tax regime involved a two-tier system: a gradually increasing rate of tax to 1100frs, applied on all cars up to an engine size of 16CV and then a flat rate of tax of 5000frs applied to any car with an engine size over 16CV. France did not produce any cars with an engine size over 16CV.

> JUDGMENT
>
> 10 The Commission considers that the special tax is contrary to the first paragraph of Art 95 of the Treaty. It argues that all cars, irrespective of their power rating for tax purposes, are similar within the meaning of the case-law of the court. That being so, it is no longer possible for a Member State to create discrimination between imported and domestically-produced vehicles. The only exception is where a Member State taxes products differently - even identical products - on the basis of neutral criteria consistent with objectives of economic policy which are compatible with the Treaty, whilst avoiding discrimination between domestic and imported products. The Commission contends, however, that the criterion adopted by France in this instance, namely power rating for tax purposes, and is not geared to an economic policy objective, such as heavier taxation of luxury products or vehicles with high fuel consumption. Accordingly, the Commission considers that the special tax, which is almost five times the highest rate of differential tax, affects imported vehicles only and does not pursue an economic policy objective compatible with the Treaty, is contrary to the first paragraph of Art 95 of the Treaty.

11 The United Kingdom government considers that vehicles of more than 16 CV are in a competitive relationship with some cars with a lower power rating for tax purposes, from which it follows that the special tax is contrary to the second paragraph of Art 95 of the Treaty since it diverts consumers from imported cars to French prestige models.

12 It is appropriate in the first place to stress that as community law stands at present the Member States are at liberty to subject products such as cars to a system of road tax which increases progressively in amount depending on an objective criterion, such as the power rating for tax purposes, which may be determined in various ways.

13 Such a system of domestic taxation is, however, compatible with Art. 95 only in so far as it is free from any discriminatory or protective effect.

14 That is not true of a system like the one at issue in the main proceedings. Under that system there are two distinct taxes: a differential tax which increases progressively and is charged on cars not exceeding a given power rating for tax purposes and a fixed tax on cars exceeding that rating which is almost five times as high as the highest rate of the differential tax. Although the system embodies no formal distinction based on the origin of products it manifestly exhibits discriminatory or protective features contrary to Art. 95, since the power rating determining liability to the special tax has been fixed at a level such that only imported cars, in particular from other Member States, are subject to the special tax whereas all cars of domestic manufacture are liable to the distinctly more advantageous differential tax.

Alert

Where discrimination is indirect it may still be permitted if it is objectively justifiable. This is an important difference between direct and indirect forms of discrimination arising from systems of internal taxation. The court has not had to deal with many cases within this category to date. One example is *Commission v Greece* Case 132/88 [1991] 3 CMLR 1.

Commission v Greece Case 132/88 [1991] 3 CMLR 1

Panel: Due CJ, Kakouris and Zuleeg PPC, Joliet, Moitinho de Almeida, Rodríguez Iglesias and Grévisse JJ. M. Jean Mischo, Advocate-General

Legislation: Art 110 (ex Art 90)

Facts: The Greek government imposed a higher tax on bigger cars, all of which were imported. However, the increase in the rate of tax was gradual and not hugely above the rate charged on smaller cars.

JUDGMENT

9 On 15 December 1986, the Hellenic Republic replied that it contested the complaints made by the Commission. It contended that both the special consumption tax and the single supplementary special tax affected domestically produced cars and those manufactured abroad without distinction, on the basis of an objective criterion, that of cylinder capacity. It stated that in Greece cars of a cylinder capacity over 1800 cc were regarded as luxury products, exclusively for people with extremely high incomes, and that it was therefore legitimate to subject them to particularly heavy taxation.

Moreover, in view of the poor infrastructure of the road network and the problems of pollution prevailing in Greece, tax legislation discouraging the purchase of large-engined cars was justified. The Hellenic Republic also pointed out the increase in taxes became steeper not only above 1 800 cc but also above 1 200 cc. Since most of the cars produced in Greece had a cylinder capacity of 1 300 cc, it was apparent that the taxes in question were not designed to protect domestic production.

10 The Commission, in its reasoned opinion of 21 September 1987, and the Hellenic Republic, in its reply thereto of 30 November 1987, maintained their respective positions.

11 Reference is made to the Report for the Hearing for a fuller account of the national legislation, the course of the procedure and the submissions and arguments of the parties, which are mentioned or discussed hereinafter only in so far as is necessary for the reasoning of the Court. ...

16 With regard to that complaint, the Hellenic Republic contended in the course of the written procedure that the differential thresholds adopted for the two taxes in question, namely 1200 cc and 1800 cc, were objectively justified because they reflected the social circumstances prevailing in Greece and, to some extent, in Europe as a whole: cars of less than 1200 cc are for people with modest incomes; those with a cylinder capacity of between 1201 and 1800 cc are bought by people whose income is in the middle range; and those of above 1800 cc are, above all in Greece, only for people with very substantial incomes.

17 It must be emphasized in this regard that Art. 95 of the Treaty does not provide a basis for censuring the excessiveness of the level of taxation which the Member States might adopt for particular products in the light of considerations of social policy. As the Court held in particular in *Humblot*, cited above, paragraphs 12 and 13, and in the judgment of 16 December 1986 in Case 200/85 *Commission v Italy* ((1986)) ECR 3953, paragraphs 8 and 10, as Community law stands at present, the Member States are at liberty to subject products such as cars to a system of tax which increases progressively in amount according to an objective criterion, such as cylinder capacity, provided that the system of taxation is free from any discriminatory or protective effect.

18 It must be made clear that a system of taxation cannot be regarded as discriminatory solely because only imported products, in particular those from other Member States, come within the most heavily taxed category (see judgment of 14 January 1981 in Case 140/79 *Chemial Farmaceutici v DAF* ((1981)) ECR 1, paragraph 18).

19 In order to determine whether the special consumption tax and the single supplementary special tax have a discriminatory or protective effect, it is necessary to consider whether they are capable of discouraging consumers from purchasing cars of a cylinder capacity in excess of 1800 cc, which are all manufactured abroad, in such a way as to benefit domestically produced cars.

20 If it is assumed that the particular features of the system of taxation at issue actually discourage certain consumers from purchasing cars of a cylinder capacity greater than

Alert

1800 cc, those consumers will choose either a model in the range of cars having cylinder capacities between 1600 and 1800 cc or a model in the range of cars having cylinder capacities below 1600 cc. All the models in the first-mentioned range are of foreign manufacture. The second range includes cars of both foreign and Greek manufacture. Consequently, the Commission has not shown how the system of taxation at issue might have the effect of favouring the sale of cars of Greek manufacture.

2.5 Non-Similar Products: Art 110 (ex Art 90)

It is possible for non-similar good to compete with each other. If an importer is able to point to goods produced within a member state which are non-similar, but compete with the goods of the importer and which enjoy some form of beneficial treatment as a result of the internal tax regime within that Member State, the importer may have a valid case against that Member State. The following case provides a useful demonstration of the approach taken when reviewing non-similar products.

Commission v UK (the *Wine and Beer* case) Case 170/78 [1983] 3 CMLR 512

Panel: Mertens de Wilmars CJ; Pescatore, O'Keeffe and Everling PPC; Lord Mackenzie Stuart, Bosco, Koopmans, Due, Bahlmann, Galmot and Kakouris JJ. Herr Gerhard Reischl and Mr. Pieter Van Loren Van Thematt, Advocates-General

Legislation: Art 110 (ex Art 90)

Facts: The UK tax system imposed a tax on wine that, if judged by equal volume (rather than straight alcohol content), was about four times that of beer. The Commission argued that this provided indirect support to the UK beer industry.

JUDGMENT

25 The Commission's calculations, which relate to the United Kingdom market in its present state and the relevance of which is not challenged by the United Kingdom government, show that wine is subject to an additional tax burden of around 58% and 77%, whereas the Italian government's calculations relating to the cheapest wine show that wine is subject to an additional tax burden of up to 286%. Those findings are indirectly confirmed by the United Kingdom government's analysis of the selling prices of the two German wines. Indeed, one of those two wines represents almost exactly the point of parity between beer and wine, from the point of view of the incidence of taxation on the price. That example shows that all cheaper wines marketed in the United Kingdom are taxed, by reference to price, more heavily in relative terms than beer. It appears from the price lists provided by the Commission that on the United Kingdom market there are an appreciable number of wines falling within that definition, and among them practically all the Italian wines, which are therefore subject to an additional tax burden which increases in inverse proportion to their price.

26 After considering the information provided by the parties, the court has come to the conclusion that, if a comparison is made on the basis of those wines which are cheaper than the types of wine selected by the United Kingdom and of which several varieties

 Alert

are sold in significant quantities on the United Kingdom market, it becomes apparent that precisely those wines which, in view of their price, are most directly in competition with domestic beer production are subject to a considerably higher tax burden.

27 It is clear, therefore, following the detailed inquiry conducted by the court - whatever criterion for comparison is used, there being no need to express a preference for one or the other - that the United Kingdom's tax system has the effect of subjecting wine imported from other Member States to an additional tax burden so as to afford protection to domestic beer production, inasmuch as beer production constitutes the most relevant reference criterion from the point of view of competition. Since such protection is most marked in the case of the most popular wines, the effect of the United Kingdom tax system is to stamp wine with the hallmarks of a luxury product which, in view of the tax burden which it bears, can scarcely constitute in the eyes of the consumer a genuine alternative to the typical domestically produced beverage.

28 It follows from the foregoing considerations that, by levying excise duty on still light wines made from fresh grapes at a higher rate, in relative terms, than on beer, the United Kingdom has failed to fulfil its obligations under the second paragraph of Article 95 of the EEC Treaty

3 Non-Fiscal Barriers

Free Movement of Goods II – Arts. 34 – 36 (formerly Arts. 28 – 30) EC

Whereas Art. 30 EC and Art 110 deal with fiscal measures which affect trade between Member States, Arts. 34-36 EC deal with non-fiscal measures, i.e. measures other than customs duties, CEE's and internal taxation. Such measures can take a wide range of forms. In addition, by their nature customs duties, CEE's and internal taxation can only be put in place by a government. In contrast, non-fiscal measures can also be put in place by non-governmental organisations. For instance a pressure group could implement a road blockade to further its cause. In such cases the member state Government can be liable for failing to take appropriate action against the relevant parties within their territory.

Art. 34 EC: Restrictions on Imports

 "Quantative restrictions on imports and all measures having equivalent effect shall be prohibited between Member States."

It is possible to break Art. 34 down into two categories, Quantitative restrictions and Measures having equivalent effect.

Quantitative Restrictions

Quantitative restrictions were defined by the ECJ in (Case 2/73) Geddo v Ente Nazionale Risi Case 2/73 1973 ECR 865.

(Case 2/73) Geddo v Ente Nazionale Risi Case 2/73 1973 ECR 865,

JUDGMENT:

7 The ban on any quantitative restriction or measure having equivalent effect in Art. 20 (2) of the said regulation has among its objects to prevent Member States from taking unilateral measures to limit exports to third countries unless otherwise permitted by the regulations.

The prohibition of such a measure as between members of the community in Art. 23 is intended to ensure the free movement of goods within the community.

The prohibition on quantitative restrictions covers measures which amount to a total or partial restraint of, according to the circumstances, imports, exports or goods in transit

Such measures usually take the form of bans or quotas on imports. Such behaviour may be justified under Art. 36 EC which is discussed further below. Otherwise it will constitute a breach of Art. 34.

3.1 Measures Having Equivalent Effect

Measures Having Equivalent Effect ('**MEQRs**') are non-fiscal disguised barriers to trade. They often take the form of requirements a product must comply with before it can be sold within a member state. The jurisprudence in this area is fairly complex. That is because there are a large number of ways in which a member state can impose MEQR's and by definition they are not necessarily obvious on the face of the provision. In addition, this area more than any other within free movement of goods, steps on the toes of the traditions and customs of the various Member States. The most heated arguments have centred on matters of food and drink, especially alcohol!

Before considering the case law in this area students should be familiar with the content of Directive 70/50. Although no longer in force this Directive heavily influenced the courts in the cases reviewed below in their assessment of MEQR's.

The most important early decision in relation to MEQR's, and the decision which defines what constitutes an MEQR is *Procureur du Roi v Benoit and Gustave Dassonville Case 8/74 1974 ECR 837.*

Procureur du Roi v Benoit and Gustave Dassonville Case 8/74 1974 ECR 837,

Facts: The Belgium law imposed a rule preventing the sale of certain products, such as Scotch whisky, without a certificate of authenticity. A trader in whisky purchased his whisky in France and made his own certificate of authenticity. The trader was accused of forging the certificate. The trader argued that the requirement for a certificate amounted to a quantitative restriction on trade

JUDGMENT:

5 All trading rules enacted by Member States which are capable of hindering, directly or indirectly, actually or potentially, intra-community trade are to be considered as measures having an effect equivalent to quantitative restrictions.

6 In the absence of a community system guaranteeing for consumers the authenticity of a product's designation of origin, if a Member State takes measures to prevent unfair practices in this connexion, it is however subject to the condition that these measures should be reasonable and that the means of proof required should not act as a hindrance to trade between Member States and should, in consequence, be accessible to all community nationals.

7 Even without having to examine whether or not such measures are covered by Art. 36, they must not, in any case, by virtue of the principle expressed in the second sentence of that Art., constitute a means of arbitrary discrimination or a disguised restriction on trade between Member States.

8 That may be the case with formalities, required by a Member State for the purpose of proving the origin of a product, which only direct importers are really in a position to satisfy without facing serious difficulties.

9 Consequently, the requirement by a Member State of a certificate of authenticity which is less easily obtainable by importers of an authentic product which has been put into free circulation in a regular manner in another Member State than by importers of the same product coming directly from the country of origin constitutes a measure having an effect equivalent to a quantitative restriction as prohibited by the Treaty.

Alert

In the now redundant Directive 70/50, the Commission signified that two types of MEQR's exist. The groups identified were distinctly and indistinctly applicable measures. Distinctly applicable measures are measures that do not apply equally to domestic and imported goods. As a result it is usually reasonably obvious that the measure adds cost to the imported product. Indistinctly applicable measures appear on their face to be equally applicable to domestic and imported goods. However, once analysed carefully the effect is to disadvantage imported goods and the reason for the measure cannot be justified. Often such measures require compliance with domestic rules which are not necessary and with which producers within the relevant member state are used to complying with in any case.

3.2 Distinctly Applicable MEQR's

In *(Case 251/78) Firma Denkavit Futtermittel GmbH v Minister für Ernährung [1979] ECR 3369* ('**Denkavit**') the ECJ considered a requirement that imported goods should be inspected to breach the prohibition as it added cost to the product because of the delay and extra transport requirements. It is easy to see the parallels between this measure and CEE's which are prohibited under Art. 30. It is possible that a member state could breach both Art. 30 and 28, by imposing an inspection (in breach of

Art. 34) and charging for that inspection (in breach of Art. 30), as was the case in Denkavit.

Facts: An importer of animal foodstuffs from the Netherlands into Germany faced an inspection regime at the border.

JUDGMENT

1. The concept of a measure having an effect equivalent to quantitative restrictions covers national measures such as those provided for by Arts. 1, 2 and 9 of the North Rhine-Westphalian regulation of 18 September 1957 relating to animal health measures applicable on the importation and transit of feeding-stuffs containing products of animal origin from abroad. Such measures fall within the prohibition in Art. 30 of the EEC Treaty unless they fall within the exception provided for by Art. 36 of the EEC Treaty.

Whereas a quota, restriction or ban is a clear form of Quantitative Restriction, a distinctly applicable measure which has the equivalent effect will by its very nature be more subtle. As a result the ECJ must carry out a careful assessment of the provision. However, it is important to note that the Dassonville formula does not require the Commission or courts to show that any particular MEQR actually hindered trade. It is enough that the measure could hinder trade.

An example of the application of these principles by the ECJ can be seen in *(Case 249/81) Commission v Ireland [1982] ECR 4005*. The case involved the promotion of domestic products by the state. The case considered whether a non-binding state promotion of good produced within a member state could breach the prohibition.

(Case 249/81) Commission v Ireland [1982] ECR 4005 ('Buy Irish'),

Facts: The Irish Government sought to promote the sale of Irish goods encouraging the use of a "Buy Irish" symbol on Irish made goods and by the organisation of a publicity campaign.

JUDGMENT

21 The Irish Government maintains that the prohibition against measures having an effect equivalent to quantitative restrictions in Art. 30 is concerned only with "measures", that is to say, binding provisions emanating from a public authority. However, no such provision has been adopted by the Irish government, which has confined itself to giving moral support and financial aid to the activities pursued by the Irish industries.

22 The Irish Government goes on to emphasize that the campaign has had no restrictive effect on imports since the proportion of Irish goods to all goods sold on the Irish market fell from 49.2% in 1977 to 43.4% in 1980.

23 The first observation to be made is that the campaign cannot be likened to advertising by private or public undertakings, or by a group of undertakings, to encourage people to buy goods produced by those undertakings. Regardless of the means used to implement it, the campaign is a reflection of the Irish Government' s

considered intention to substitute domestic products for imported products on the Irish market and thereby to check the flow of imports from other Member States.

24 It must be remembered here that a representative of the Irish Government stated when the campaign was launched that it was a carefully thought-out set of initiatives constituting an integrated programme for promoting domestic products; that the Irish goods council was set up at the initiative of the Irish Government a few months later; and that the task of implementing the integrated programme as it was envisaged by the Government was entrusted, or left, to that council.

25 Whilst it may be true that the two elements of the programme which have continued in effect, namely the advertising campaign and the use of the "guaranteed Irish" symbol, have not had any significant success in winning over the Irish market to domestic products, it is not possible to overlook the fact that, regardless of their efficacy, those two activities form part of a Government programme which is designed to achieve the substitution of domestic products for imported products and is liable to affect the volume of trade between Member States.

26 The advertising campaign to encourage the sale and purchase of Irish products cannot be divorced from its origin as part of the Government programme, or from its connection with the introduction of the "Guaranteed Irish" symbol and with the organization of a special system for investigating complaints about products bearing that symbol. The establishment of the system for investigating complaints about Irish products provides adequate confirmation of the degree of organization surrounding the "Buy Irish" 'campaign and of the discriminatory nature of the campaign.

27 In the circumstances the two activities in question amount to the establishment of a national practice, introduced by the Irish Government and prosecuted with its assistance, the potential effect of which on imports from other Member States is comparable to that resulting from Government measures of a binding nature.

28 Such a practice cannot escape the prohibition laid down by Art. 30 of the Treaty solely because it is not based on decisions which are binding upon undertakings. Even measures adopted by the Government of a member state which do not have binding effect may be capable of influencing the conduct of traders and consumers in that state and thus of frustrating the aims of the community as set out in Art. 2 and enlarged upon in Art. 3 of the Treaty.

29 That is the case where, as in this instance, such a restrictive practice represents the implementation of a programme defined by the Government which affects the national economy as a whole and which is intended to check the flow of trade between Member States by encouraging the purchase of domestic products, by means of an advertising campaign on a national scale and the organization of special procedures applicable solely to domestic products, and where those activities are attributable as a whole to the Government and are pursued in an organized fashion throughout the national territory.

30 Ireland has therefore failed to fulfil its obligations under the Treaty by organizing a campaign to promote the sale and purchase of Irish goods within its territory.

3.3 Indistinctly Applicable MEQR's

Indistinctly applicable measures are the most subtle form of provision prohibited under Art. 34. Many of the cases involve packaging and presentation rules. Some rules and requirements pre-dated the entry of the relevant member state into the union and sometimes reflected particular traditions of that member state. However, an important component of the enforcement of Art. 34 was the removal of these rules where they could not be justified. The ECJ confirmed that such rules are capable of infringing Art. 34 in the seminal decision in *(Case 120/78) Rewe-Zentrale AG v Bundesmonopolverwaltung fur Branntwein [1979] ECR 649* ('**Cassis de Dijon**')

(Case 120/78) Rewe-Zentrale AG v Bundesmonopolverwaltung fur Branntwein [1979] ECR 649,

Facts: An importer wanted to import the liqueur "Cassis de Dijon" from Germany into France. German law specified that such liqueurs had to have an alcohol content of 25 per cent. Cassis de Dijon had an alcohol content of between 15 and 20 per cent and therefore it importation into Germany was not permitted.

JUDGMENT

6 The national court is thereby asking for assistance in the matter of interpretation in order to enable it to assess whether the requirement of a minimum alcohol content may be covered either by the prohibition on all measures having an effect equivalent to quantitative restrictions in trade between Member States contained in Art. 30 of the Treaty or by the prohibition on all discrimination regarding the conditions under which goods are procured and marketed between nationals of Member States within the meaning of Art. 37.

7 It should be noted in this connexion that Art. 37 relates specifically to state monopolies of a commercial character.

That provision is therefore irrelevant with regard to national provisions which do not concern the exercise by a public monopoly of its specific function - namely, it's exclusive right - but apply in a general manner to the production and marketing of alcoholic beverages, whether or not the latter are covered by the monopoly in question.

That being the case, the effect on intra-community trade of the measure referred to by the national court must be examined solely in relation to the requirements under Art. 30, as referred to by the first question.

...

[The ECJ then discussed possible justification for the measure, and in so doing provided the seminal part of the judgement which set out the rule of reason. This part of the judgement is extracted and discussed further below. In conclusion the ECJ then stated:]

15 Consequently, the first question should be answered to the effect that the concept of "measures having an effect equivalent to quantitative restrictions on imports " contained in Art. 30 of the Treaty is to be understood to mean that the fixing of a minimum

alcohol content for alcoholic beverages intended for human consumption by the legislation of a Member State also falls within the prohibition laid down in that provision where the importation of alcoholic beverages lawfully produced and marketed in another member state is concerned.

An example of the application of Art. 34 in relation to a form of packaging that had become "traditional" in a particular Member State can be found in (Case 261/81) Walter Rau Lebensmittelwerke v Smedt PvbA [1982] ECR 3961.

(Case 261/81) Walter Rau Lebensmittelwerke v Smedt PvbA [1982] ECR 3961,

Facts: Belgian statute required all margarine in Belgium to be sold in cubic packages. The Belgian Government argued that this applied to all sellers of margarine and the measure was in place to avoid customer confusion. One of the questions the ECJ considered is whether customers could be informed in other ways rather than just by standard packaging.

JUDGMENT

The application in one Member State to margarine imported from another Member State and lawfully produced and marketed in that state of legislation prohibiting the marketing of margarine or edible fats where each block or its external packaging does not have a particular shape, for example the shape of a cube, in circumstances in which the consumer may be protected and informed by means which hinder the free movement of goods to a lesser degree constitutes a measure having an effect equivalent to a quantitative restriction within the meaning of Art. 30 of the Treaty

Another example of the courts identifying an indistinctly applicable MEQR can be found in the case of (Case 45/87) Commission v Ireland [1988] ECR 4929.

(Case 45/87) Commission v Ireland [1988] ECR 4929,

Facts: Contractors tendering for the contract to supply water to Dundalk, whether from Ireland or elsewhere, were required by the Irish Government to supply pipes which complied with 'Irish Standard Mark 188'. Only one manufacturer made such pipes and it was Irish. One contractor argued it should be allowed to bid using pipes that met an international standard as they would do the same job.

JUDGMENT

21 The Irish Government maintains that it is necessary to specify the standards to which materials must be manufactured, particularly in a case such as this where the pipes utilized must suit the existing network. Compliance with another standard, even an international standard such as ISO 160:1980, would not suffice to eliminate certain technical difficulties.

22 That technical argument cannot be accepted. The Commission's complaint does not relate to compliance with technical requirements but to the refusal of the Irish authorities to verify whether those requirements are satisfied where the manufacturer of the

materials has not been certified by the IIRS to IS 188. By incorporating in the notice in question the words "or equivalent" after the reference to the Irish standard, as provided for by Directive 71/305 where it is applicable, the Irish authorities could have verified compliance with the technical conditions without from the outset restricting the contract only to tenderers proposing to utilize Irish materials.

3.4 Defences

Art. 36 sets out the defences available to Member States in respect of a potential breach of Art. 34. The defences are available in respect of both QR's and MEQR's. Additional defences are available in respect of indistinctly applicable MEQR's under the 'rule of reason' as described further below.

3.4.1 – Art. 36 Derogations

Art. 36 sets out 6 derogations: public morality; public policy; public security; the protection of health and life of humans, animals or plants; the protection of national treasures possessing artistic, historic or archaeological value and finally the protection of industrial and commercial property. Set out below are cases two of the most used derogations, Public Morality and The protection of health and life of humans, animals or plants.

Public Morality

(Case 121/85) Conegate Ltd v Commissioners of Customs and Excise,

Note: Art. 177 is now Art. 267

Facts: The UK sought to prevent the import of life-size inflatable 'love-love' dolls from Germany. The production of such dolls was legal within the UK.

JUDGMENT

15 However, although community law leaves the Member States free to make their own assessments of the indecent or obscene character of certain articles, it must be pointed out that the fact that goods cause offence cannot be regarded as sufficiently serious to justify restrictions on the free movement of goods where the member state concerned does not adopt, with respect to the same goods manufactured or marketed within its territory, penal measures or other serious and effective measures intended to prevent the distribution of such goods in its territory.

16 It follows that a Member State may not rely on grounds of public morality in order to prohibit the importation of goods from other Member States when its legislation contains no prohibition on the manufacture or marketing of the same goods on its territory.

17 It is not for the court, within the framework of the powers conferred upon it by Art. 177 of the EEC Treaty, to consider whether, and to what extent, the United Kingdom legislation contains such a prohibition. However, the question whether or not such a prohibition exists in a state comprised of different constituent parts which have their

Alert

own internal legislation, can be resolved only by taking into consideration all the relevant legislation. Although it is not necessary, for the purposes of the application of the above-mentioned rule, that the manufacture and marketing of the products whose importation has been prohibited should be prohibited in the territory of all the constituent parts, it must at least be possible to conclude from the applicable rules, taken as a whole, that their purpose is, in substance, to prohibit the manufacture and marketing of those products.

18 In this instance, in the actual wording of its first question the high court took care to define the substance of the national legislation the compatibility of which with community law is a question which it proposes to determine. Thus it refers to rules in the importing Member State under which the goods in question may be manufactured freely and marketed subject only to certain restrictions, which it sets out explicitly, namely an absolute prohibition on the transmission of such goods by post, a restriction on their public display and, in certain areas of the Member State concerned, a system of licensing of premises for the sale of those goods to customers aged 18 years and over. Such restrictions cannot however be regarded as equivalent in substance to a prohibition on manufacture and marketing.

The protection of health and life of humans, animals or plants

(Case 174/82) Officer van Justice v Santoz BV [1983] ECR 2445,

Facts: The Dutch authorities refused to allow the sale of muesli bars containing added vitamins on the grounds that excessive consumption of vitamins could be harmful to human health. Scientific data did not provide a clear answer as to the point at which vitamins did become harmful to health.

JUDGMENT

16 As the court found in its judgment of 17 December 1981 in Case 272/80 (Frans-nederlandse Maatschappij Voor Biologische Producten (1981) ECR 3277), in so far as there are uncertainties at the present state of scientific research it is for the Member States, in the absence of harmonization, to decide what degree of protection of the health and life of humans they intend to assure, having regard however for the requirements of the free movement of goods within the community.

17 Those principles also apply to substances such as vitamins which are not as a general rule harmful in themselves but may have special harmful effects solely if taken to excess as part of the general nutrition, the composition of which is unforeseeable and cannot be monitored. In view of the uncertainties inherent in the scientific assessment, national rules prohibiting, without prior authorization, the marketing of foodstuffs to which vitamins have been added are justified on principle within the meaning of Art. 36 of the Treaty on grounds of the protection of human health.

18 Nevertheless the principle of proportionality which underlies the last sentence of Art. 36 of the Treaty requires that the power of the Member States to prohibit imports of the products in question from other Member States should be restricted to what is necessary to attain the legitimate aim of protecting health. Accordingly, national rules providing

 Alert

for such a prohibition are justified only if authorizations to market are granted when they are compatible with the need to protect health.

19 Such an assessment is, however, difficult to make in relation to additives such as vitamins the abovementioned characteristics of which exclude the possibility of foreseeing or monitoring the quantities consumed as part of the general nutrition and the degree of harmfulness of which cannot be determined with sufficient certainty. Nevertheless, although in view of the present stage of harmonization of national laws at the community level a wide discretion must be left to the Member States, they must, in order to observe the principle of proportionality, authorize marketing when the addition of vitamins to foodstuffs meets a real need, especially a technical or nutritional one.

20 The first question must therefore be answered to the effect that community law permits national rules prohibiting without prior authorization the marketing of foodstuffs lawfully marketed in another Member State to which vitamins have been added, provided that the marketing is authorized when the addition of vitamins meets a real need, especially a technical or nutritional one.

Second question

21 In the second question the national court asks in essence whether community law precludes national rules such as those referred to by the national court where the authorization to market is subject to proof by the importer that the product in question is not harmful to health.

22 In as much as the question arises as to where the onus of proof lies when there is a request for authorization, in view of the answer to the first question, it must be remembered that Art. 36 of the Treaty creates an exception, which must be strictly interpreted, to the rule of free movement of goods within the community which is one of the fundamental principles of the common market. It is therefore for the national authorities who rely on that provision in order to adopt a measure restricting intra-community trade to check in each instance that the measure contemplated satisfies the criteria of that provision.

23 Accordingly, although the national authorities may, in so far as they do not have it themselves, ask the importer to produce the information in his possession relating to the composition of the product and the technical or nutritional reasons for adding vitamins, they must themselves assess, in the light of all the relevant information, whether authorization must be granted pursuant to community law.

Alert

24 The second question must therefore be answered to the effect that community law does not permit national rules which subject authorization to market to proof by the importer that the product in question is not harmful to health, without prejudice to the right of the national authorities to ask the importer to submit all the information in his possession needed to assess the facts

3.5 – The 'Rule of Reason'

The ECJ allowed additional defences in respect of indistinctly applicable MEQR's in Cassis de Dijon. The concept of wider defences for such measures is attractive partly because a measure that does not distinguish between goods produced with a member state and those which are imported may be 'objectively justified' by wider criteria than those set out in Art. 36. It is for this reason that the ECJ set out 'mandatory requirements' in its seminal judgement in Cassis de Dijon. The mandatory requirements are effectively additional defences available in the case of an indistinctly applicable MEQR. It must be remembered however that the mandatory requirements must be balanced against the presumption of mutual recognition.

(Case 120/78) Rewe-Zentrale AG v Bundesmonopolverwaltung fur Branntwein [1979] ECR 649,

JUDGMENT

In the absence of common rules relating to the production and marketing of alcohol - a proposal for a regulation submitted to the council by the Commission on 7 December 1976 (Official Journal C309, P.2) not yet having received the council's approval - it is for the Member States to regulate all matters relating to the production and marketing of alcohol and alcoholic beverages on their own territory.

Obstacles to movement within the community resulting from disparities between the national laws relating to the marketing of the products in question must be accepted in so far as those provisions may be recognized as being necessary in order to satisfy mandatory requirements relating in particular to the effectiveness of fiscal supervision, the protection of public health, the fairness of commercial transactions and the defence of the consumer.

Alert

9 The Government of the federal republic of Germany, intervening in the proceedings, put forward various arguments which, in its view, justify the application of provisions relating to the minimum alcohol content of alcoholic beverages, adducing considerations relating on the one hand to the protection of public health and on the other to the protection of the consumer against unfair commercial practices.

10 As regards the protection of public health the German Government states that the purpose of the fixing of minimum alcohol contents by national legislation is to avoid the proliferation of alcoholic beverages on the national market, in particular alcoholic beverages with a low alcohol content, since, in its view, such products may more easily induce a tolerance towards alcohol than more highly alcoholic beverages.

11 Such considerations are not decisive since the consumer can obtain on the market an extremely wide range of weakly or moderately alcoholic products and furthermore a large proportion of alcoholic beverages with a high alcohol content freely sold on the German market is generally consumed in a diluted form.

12 The German Government also claims that the fixing of a lower limit for the alcohol content of certain liqueurs is designed to protect the consumer against unfair practices on the part of producers and distributors of alcoholic beverages.

This argument is based on the consideration that the lowering of the alcohol content secures a competitive advantage in relation to beverages with a higher alcohol content, since alcohol constitutes by far the most expensive constituent of beverages by reason of the high rate of tax to which it is subject.

Furthermore, according to the German government, to allow alcoholic products into free circulation wherever, as regards their alcohol content, they comply with the rules laid down in the country of production would have the effect of imposing as a common standard within the community the lowest alcohol content permitted in any of the Member States, and even of rendering any requirements in this field inoperative since a lower limit of this nature is foreign to the rules of several Member States.

13 As the Commission rightly observed, the fixing of limits in relation to the alcohol content of beverages may lead to the standardization of products placed on the market and of their designations, in the interests of a greater transparency of commercial transactions and offers for sale to the public.

However, this line of argument cannot be taken so far as to regard the mandatory fixing of minimum alcohol contents as being an essential guarantee of the fairness of commercial transactions, since it is a simple matter to ensure that suitable information is conveyed to the purchaser by requiring the display of an indication of origin and of the alcohol content on the packaging of products.

14 It is clear from the foregoing that the requirements relating to the minimum alcohol content of alcoholic beverages do not serve a purpose which is in the general interest and such as to take precedence over the requirements of the free movement of goods, which constitutes one of the fundamental rules of the community.

In practice, the principle effect of requirements of this nature is to promote alcoholic beverages having a high alcohol content by excluding from the national market products of other Member States which do not answer that description.

It therefore appears that the unilateral requirement imposed by the rules of a member state of minimum alcohol content for the purposes of the sale of alcoholic beverages constitutes an obstacle to trade which is incompatible with the provisions of Art. 30 of the Treaty.

There is therefore no valid reason why, provided that they have been lawfully produced and marketed in one of the Member States, alcoholic beverages should not be introduced into any other member state; the sale of such products may not be subject to a legal prohibition on the marketing of beverages with an alcohol content lower than the limit set by the national rules.

 Alert

3.6 Post Cassis de Dijon

The judgment in Cassis de Dijon is not without controversy. Some question the need for additional defences beyond those set out in Art. 36. Subsequent case law made it clear that the principle of mutual recognition would often provide a useful weapon for the importer. However, the courts have not treated the list of mandatory requirements

Law of the European Union

set out in Cassis de Dijon as an exhaustive list. Therefore, additional requirements have been permitted, such as the protection of the environment in *(Case 302/86) Commission v Denmark [1988] ECR 460.*

Governments became concerned that the principle of mutual recognition had become too strong a weapon for importers and in some cases importers were citing the principle incorrectly. The ECJ sought to deal with this concern in. *(C-267 and 268/91) Criminal Proceedings against Keck and Mithouard [1993] ECR I-6097* by distinguishing indistinctly applicable measures that actually hinder trade between Member States (which are unlawful) and indistinctly applicable measures that had an overall effect on volumes of trade, but did not affect imports more than domestic products.

(C-267 and 268/91) Criminal Proceedings against Keck and Mithouard [1993] ECR I-6097,

Note: Art. 30 is now Art. 34

Facts: Keck and Mithouard sold goods at a loss in contravention of French law. They argued that the law deprived them of a method of promoting their goods imported by them into France.

JUDGMENT

12 National legislation imposing a general prohibition on resale at a loss is not designed to regulate trade in goods between Member States.

13 Such legislation may, admittedly, restrict the volume of sales, and hence the volume of sales of products from other Member States, in so far as it deprives traders of a method of sales promotion. But the question remains whether such a possibility is sufficient to characterize the legislation in question as a measure having equivalent effect to a quantitative restriction on imports.

14 In view of the increasing tendency of traders to invoke Art. 30 of the Treaty as a means of challenging any rules whose effect is to limit their commercial freedom even where such rules are not aimed at products from other Member States, the Court considers it necessary to re-examine and clarify its case-law on this matter.

15 It is established by the case-law beginning with "Cassis de Dijon" (Case 120/78 Rewe-Zentral v Bundesmonopolverwaltung fuer Branntwein [1979] ECR 649) that, in the absence of harmonization of legislation, obstacles to free movement of goods which are the consequence of applying, to goods coming from other Member States where they are lawfully manufactured and marketed, rules that lay down requirements to be met by such goods (such as those relating to designation, form, size, weight, composition, presentation, labelling, packaging) constitute measures of equivalent effect prohibited by Art. 30. This is so even if those rules apply without distinction to all products unless their application can be justified by a public-interest objective taking precedence over the free movement of goods.

16 By contrast, contrary to what has previously been decided, the application to products from other Member States of national provisions restricting or prohibiting

Alert

certain selling arrangements is not such as to hinder directly or indirectly, actually or potentially, trade between Member States within the meaning of the Dassonville judgment (Case 8/74 [1974] ECR 837), so long as those provisions apply to all relevant traders operating within the national territory and so long as they affect in the same manner, in law and in fact, the marketing of domestic products and of those from other Member States.

17 Provided that those conditions are fulfilled, the application of such rules to the sale of products from another Member State meeting the requirements laid down by that State is not by nature such as to prevent their access to the market or to impede access any more than it impedes the access of domestic products. Such rules therefore fall outside the scope of Art. 30 of the Treaty.

18 Accordingly, the reply to be given to the national court is that Art. 30 of the EEC Treaty is to be interpreted as not applying to legislation of a Member State imposing a general prohibition on resale at a loss.

This clarification proved useful in defeating illegitimate claims from importers such as claims that Sunday trading laws could be an indistinctly applicable MEQR. In (Case 169/91) *Stoke-on-Trent and Norwich City Councils v B&Q plc [1992] ECR I-6635* the laws were found to be justified and proportionate as they did not affect imports more than domestic products.

Further Reading

Barents, R: 'Charges of Equivalent Effect to Customs Duties' (1978) 15 CMLRev 415

Chalmers, D: 'Repackaging the Internal Market – The Ramifications of the Keck Judgment' (1994) 19 ELR 385

Easson, A: 'The Spirits, Wine and Beer Judgements: A Legal Mickey Finn?' (1980) 5 ELR 318

Shuibhne, N: 'The Free Movement of Goods and Article 28: An Evolving Framework' (2002) 27 ELR 408

6

Freedom of Establishment and of Provision of Services

Topic List

Daryll Bewick

1 Freedom of Establishment

Freedom of Establishment, enshrined in Art 49 (ex Art 43), is one of the fundamental freedoms crucial to the development of the internal market. While the Free Movement of Persons largely covers the employee, Establishment covers the self-employed professional or trade person and also covers both natural and legal persons.

A unifying feature across most areas of EU law is the basic goal of achieving a level playing field.

However, there are distinguishing features unique to Establishment and Services. The most obvious of these is existence of the raft of legislation, which is indicative of the importance attached by the Treaty to both professional qualifications and the need for professional expertise to be widely available across the EU.

So we shall see that while case law began the process of 'levelling the field' it was overtaken by measures such as Directive 2005/36. As a result nearly all professions are now covered by legislation and it is this which lays down the path to be followed by Member States concerned about professional qualification. Nonetheless the case law is of seminal importance here as the legislation is based upon the case law principles. Wherever there is a gap in the legislation the case law fills it (the unregulated professions being an obvious example). Even where there is not a gap the case law defining Art 49 can still be relied upon to ensure acquisition of skills is fully taken into account.

Jean Reyners v The Belgian State Case 2/74 [1974] 2 CMLR 305

Panel: Lecourt P, Donner, Sørensen, Monaco, Mertens de Wilmars, Pescatore, Kutscher, Ó Dálaigh and Lord Mackenzie Stuart JJ. M. Henri Mayras, Advocate-General

Legislation: Art 49 (ex Art 43), Art 51 (ex Art 45), Art 59 (ex Art 52), Art 61 (ex Art 54), Art 64 (ex Art 57)

Facts: Jean Reyners was born in Brussels and spent his life in Belgium even though he was born of Dutch parents and retained Dutch nationality. In Belgium he pursued legal studies culminating in his award of Doctor of Belgian Law. Despite this he was not allowed to practise as an avocat in Belgium because he was not of Belgian nationality. This requirement could have been removed by Royal dispensation but this required the home states of such foreign nationals to display reciprocity towards Belgian nationals in similar situations in their states. Holland required Dutch nationality for its legal practitioners. Reyners applied a number of times for the Royal dispensation arguing the Belgian requirement was contrary to the Treaty of Rome.

The Belgian Conseil d'Etat sent a preliminary reference to the ECJ, asking two questions:

The key question was whether the profession of avocat was exempt from the Treaty on the basis of Art 51 (ex Art 45) which allowed 'activities which in that State are connected, even occasionally, with the exercise of official authority' to be excluded from the provisions of the Treaty. Particularly did this refer only to those aspects of an avocat's role which required them to exercise official authority or was it referring to the role of avocat per se?

ADVOCATE-GENERAL M HENRY MAYRAS.

The Advocate General began by explaining the purpose behind Art 49 (ex Art 43):

> The economic integration which is the basic aim of the Rome Treaty implies the development of trade in a single market as well as the free circulation of goods and men. It opens up to undertakings and to workers a field of action widened to the whole of the Community, multiplies business relations and thus contributes to breaking down the national framework which has become too narrow.
>
> Consequently, it requires also not only that all restrictions should be abolished on the free supply of services within that Community, but also that the nationals of each member country should be recognised as having the right to establish themselves in another member-State and there to carry out their occupations, whether they be industrial, commercial, agricultural or professional, on the same conditions as the nationals of the latter State.

He argued that similar Treaty requirements for transitional periods for the attainment of some of the other Freedoms had not stopped the court establishing direct effect:

> The Treaty offers many examples of provisions using the same techniques, whether for the abolition of customs duties on imports (Article 13) or on exports (Article 16) between the member-States, or the prohibition on member-States subjecting the goods of other member-States, either directly or indirectly, to internal taxes of any nature higher than those to which similar national products are subject. In these various cases the obligations imposed on the States were to be gradually complied with: 'during the transitional period' as Article 13 says ...
>
> You have not hesitated to decide that on expiry of the term fixed in [this] case the rules laid down by [this] provision [was] to become directly applicable.
>
> You held so regarding Article 95 in *Alfons Lütticke GmbH v. Hauptzollamt Sarrelouis* (57/65).

While with regard to Art 51 (ex Art 45) the role of avocat could not be precluded per se simply because of a potential exercise of official authority. An avocat is not necessarily in a position to exercise such power. Art 51 was only designed to cover those situations where an avocat was in such a position. Such situations were likely to be limited:

> Official authority is that which derives from the sovereignty, the imperium of the state; it implies, for the one exercising it, the power to enjoy prerogatives which fall outside the ordinary law (*exorbittantes du droit commun*), privileges of public power, powers of coercion over the citizens.

The Court was to broadly fall in line with his approach. It explained its decision with regard to direct effect.

> JUDGMENT
>
> ... At the end of the transitional period, the member-States no longer have the possibility of maintaining restrictions on the freedom of establishment, since Article 52 has, as from this period, the character of a provision which is complete in itself and legally perfect.
>
> [13] In these circumstances the 'general programme' and the directives provided for by Article 54 were of significance only during the transitional period, since the freedom of establishment was fully attained at the end of it...
>
> Article 52 expresses the guiding principle in the matter by providing that freedom of establishment shall include the right to take up and pursue activities as self employed persons 'under the conditions laid down for its own nationals by the law of the country where such establishment is effected'.
>
> [19] For the purpose of achieving this objective by progressive stages during the transitional period Article 54 provides for the drawing up by the Council of a 'general programme' and, for the implementation of this programme, directives intended to attain freedom of establishment in respect of the various activities in question...
>
> [24] The rule on equal treatment with nationals is one of the fundamental legal provisions of the Community.
>
> [25] As a reference to a set of legislative provisions effectively applied by the country of establishment to its own nationals, this rule is, by its essence, capable of being directly invoked by nationals of all the other member-States.
>
> [26] In laying down that freedom of establishment shall be attained at the end of the transitional period, Article 52 thus imposes an obligation to attain a precise result, the fulfilment of which had to be made easier by, but not made dependent on, the implementation of a programme of progressive measures.
>
> [27] The fact that this progression has not been adhered to leaves the obligation itself intact beyond the end of the period provided for its fulfilment
>
> [28] This interpretation is in accordance with Article 8 (7) of the Treaty, according to which the expiry of the transitional period shall constitute the latest date by which all the rules laid down must enter into force and all the measures required for establishing the Common Market must be implemented.
>
> [29] It is not possible to invoke against such an effect the fact that the Council has failed to issue the directives provided for by Articles 54 and 57 or the fact that certain of the directives actually issued have not fully attained the objective of non-discrimination required by Article 52.
>
> [30] After the expiry of the transitional period the directives provided for by the Chapter on the right of establishment have become superfluous with regard to

implementing the rule on nationality, since this is henceforth sanctioned by the Treaty itself with direct effect.

[32] It is right therefore to reply to the question raised that, since the end of the transitional period, Article 52 of the Treaty is a directly applicable provision despite the absence in a particular sphere, of the directives prescribed by Articles 54(2) and 57(1) of the Treaty.

With regard to the second question concerning the extent of Art 51 (ex Art 45):

[34]...[T]he question is whether, within a profession such as that of *avocat*, only those activities inherent in this profession which are connected with the exercise of official authority are excepted from the application of the Chapter on the right of establishment, or whether the whole of this profession is excepted by reason of the fact that it comprises activities connected with the exercise of this authority...

[38] The plaintiff in the main action, for his part, contends that at most only certain activities of the profession of *avocat* are connected with the exercise of official authority and that they alone therefore come within the exception created by Article 55 to the principle of free establishment.

The court followed the plaintiff's line of reasoning:

... [46] An extension of the exception allowed by Article 55 to a whole profession would be possible only in cases where such activities were linked with that profession in such a way that freedom of establishment would result in imposing on the member-State concerned the obligation to allow the exercise, even occasionally, by non-nationals of functions appertaining to official authority.

[47] This extension is on the other hand not possible when, within the framework of an independent profession, the activities connected with the exercise of official authority are separable from the professional activity in question taken as a whole...

[51] Professional activities involving contacts, even regular and organic, with the courts, including even compulsory co-operation in their functioning, do not constitute, as such, connection with the exercise of official authority.

[52] The most typical activities of the profession of *avocat*, in particular, such as consultation and legal assistance and also representation and the defence of parties in court, even when the intervention or assistance of the *avocat* is compulsory or is a legal monopoly, cannot be considered as connected with the exercise of official authority.

[53] The exercise of these activities leaves the discretion of judicial authority and the free exercise of judicial power intact.

[54] It is therefore right to reply to the question raised that the exception to freedom of establishment provided for by the first paragraph of Article 55 must be restricted to those of the activities referred to in Article 52 which in themselves involve a direct and specific connection with the exercise of official authority...

Note that this was a case of direct discrimination (based upon nationality).

The Right of Establishment is given in Art 49 (ex Art 43) which removes national restrictions upon the self employed to set up and manage undertakings within the EU. Art 50 (ex Art 44) however required the Council and Commission to establish a programme for the abolition of such restrictions because the achievement of Art 50 was a necessary prerequisite to the achievement of Art 49. With Art 49 conditional upon the achievement of Art 50 it was as a result incapable of direct effect until Art 50 was achieved. Given the difficulty in getting Member State agreement to the harmonisation measures under Art 50 the direct effect of Art 49 seemed a long way off. *Reyners* was the case where the ECJ cut this particular Gordian knot.

Thieffry v Conseil de l'Ordre des Avocats à la Cour de Paris (Paris Bar Council) Case 71/76 [1977] 2 CMLR 373

Panel: Kutscher CJ, Donner and Pescatore PPC, Mertens de Wilmars, Sørensen, Lord Mackenzie Stuart, O'Keeffe, Bosco and Touffait JJ. M. Henri Mayras, Advocate-General

Legislation: Art 49 (ex Art 43) Art 53 (ex Art 47)

Facts: Jean Thieffry was of Belgian nationality and possessed a Doctor of Laws from the University of Louvain (Belgium). He subsequently practised as an advocate at the Brussels Bar for more than 10 years.

He then assisted a London barrister for a number of years before finally settling in Paris, where for some years he assisted in the chambers of an advocate of the Paris bar as well as teaching law.

He had been effectively practising the profession of advocate for about 20 years and had been offered a partnership by a Parisian advocate, subject to his becoming a member of the Paris Bar.

With the aim of being admitted to that Bar, in 1974 Mr. Thieffry obtained recognition of equivalence from the University of Paris that his Belgian qualification was equivalent to the French degree in law. He then sat and passed the qualifying certificate for the profession of advocate in 1975.

The Paris Bar rejected his application by a decision of 9 March 1976. While the Bar accepted the direct effect of Art 49, it took the view that a French doctorate in law was required and that Mr. Thieffry's application for membership had to be rejected.

JUDGMENT

[15] It follows from the provisions cited taken as a whole that freedom of establishment, subject to observance of professional rules justified by the general good, is one of the objectives of the Treaty.

[16] In so far as Community law makes no special provision, these objectives may be attained by measures enacted by the member-States, which under Article 5 of the Treaty are bound to take 'all appropriate measures, whether general or particular, to ensure fulfilment of the obligations arising out of this Treaty or resulting from action

taken by the institutions of the Community', and to abstain 'from any measure which could jeopardise the attainment of the objectives of this Treaty' .

[17] Consequently, if the freedom of establishment provided for by Article 52 can be ensured in a member-State either under the provisions of the laws and regulations in force, or by virtue of the practices of the public service or of professional bodies, a person subject to Community law cannot be denied the practical benefit of that freedom solely by virtue of the fact that, for a particular profession, the directives provided for by Article 57 of the Treaty have not yet been adopted.

[18] Since the practical enjoyment of freedom of establishment can thus in certain circumstances depend upon national practice or legislation, it is incumbent upon the competent public authorities—including legally recognised professional bodies—to ensure that such practice or legislation is applied in accordance with the objective defined by the provisions of the Treaty relating to freedom of establishment.

[19] In particular, there is an unjustified restriction on that freedom where, in a member-State, admission to a particular profession is refused to a person covered by the Treaty who holds a diploma which has been recognised as an equivalent qualification by the competent authority of the country of establishment and who furthermore has fulfilled the specific conditions regarding professional training in force in that country, solely by reason of the fact that the person concerned does not possess the national diploma corresponding to the diploma which he holds and which has been recognised as an equivalent qualification.

Alert

[20] The national court specifically referred to the effect of a recognition of equivalence 'by the university authority of the country of establishment', and in the course of the proceedings the question has been raised whether a distinction should be drawn, as regards the equivalence of diplomas, between university recognition, granted with a view to permitting the pursuit of certain studies, and a recognition having 'civil effect' , granted with a view to permitting the pursuit of a professional activity…

[22] Since this distinction falls within the ambit of the national law of the different States, it is for the national authorities to assess the consequences thereof, taking account, however, of the objectives of Community law…

[24]… It is for the national authorities to judge whether a recognition granted by a university authority can, in addition to its academic effect, constitute valid evidence of a professional qualification.

As seen above, the French government (rather than the Paris Bar) drew a distinction between those decisions of university authorities which have civil effects and those which have academic effects. The former confer rights upon their recipients which can be enforced even outside the university, the latter confer rights only in respect of the university institution. The recognition of diplomas in question in this case belongs to the latter category. Such recognition gives the right to follow studies from one university to another, but does not involve any civil effect, in particular the right to practise a profession. This latter aspect ought to remain in the hands of the state.

The ECJ accepted this position. While a university may establish equivalence of qualifications it is the competent host State authorities which must determine whether such university recognition shall also constitute valid evidence of professional qualification. This recognition for professional purposes was a question of fact.

[27] In these circumstances, the answer to the question referred to the Court should be that when a national of one member-State desirous of exercising a professional activity such as the profession of advocate in another member-State has obtained a diploma in his country of origin which has been recognised as an equivalent qualification by the competent authority under the legislation of the country of establishment and which has thus enabled him to sit and pass the special qualifying examination for the profession in question, the act of demanding the national diploma prescribed by the legislation of the country of establishment constitutes, even in the absence of the directives provided for in Article 57 , a restriction incompatible with the freedom of establishment guaranteed by Article 52 of the Treaty.

 Alert

Thieffry advanced the law beyond the point reached by *Reyners*.

In *Thieffry* the French Bar had in fact accepted the decision in *Reyners* and did not base their case upon direct discrimination (grounds of nationality) but upon an indirect discrimination argument based around the lack of an appropriate qualification (albeit a national one).

Also note that in *Reyners* the ECJ distinguished between two functions which the EU should accomplish:

▸ a negative function eliminating obstacles to freedom of establishment; and
▸ a positive function introducing laws to facilitate freedom of establishment.

This case moved a stage further by laying the ground rules for the establishment of mutual recognition of equivalent qualifications (the positive function) even where there was no legislation establishing this yet.

The court established within the context of Establishment that where a State measure is indirectly discriminatory then it must be objectively justifiable by the State as well as being a proportionate reaction. This approach was to be followed and built upon in subsequent case law.

Reinhard Gebhard v Consiglio Dell'Ordine degli Avvocati E Procuratori di Milano Case 55/94 [1996] 1 CMLR 603

Panel: Rodríguez Iglesias P, Kakouris, Edward (Rapporteur), and Hirsch PPC, Mancini, Schockweiler, Moitinho de Almeida, Kapteyn, Gulmann, Murray, Jann, Ragnemalm and Sevon JJ. M. Philippe Léger, Advocate-General

Legislation: Art 49 (ex Art 43)

Facts: Reinhard Gebhard was a German national and law graduate of the University of Tubingen. In 1977 he was authorised to practise as a member of the Stuttgart Bar in Germany. He married an Italian national and settled in Italy with three children in 1978 where he worked as an associate member of a lawyers chambers in Milan before going on to practise as an Avvocato (lawyer) in his own chambers. His work was non contentious with 65% of his turnover derived from assisting and representing German speakers, 35% from assisting Italians in Germany and Austria and 5% from assisting Italian lawyers dealing with problems of German law. His work was essentially advisory about non-Italian law and when it came to the application of Italian law or court work in Italy he had recourse to Italian practitioners.

In 1992 the Milan Bar denied him the right to use the title of Avvocato from a permanent basis of chambers in Italy in contravention of Italian law and suspended him from acting as a lawyer for six months.

He appealed these findings and preliminary references were made to the ECJ concerning how compliant Italian law was with the Treaty and what criteria could be used to distinguish a provider of services from a lawyer established in a Member State.

ADVOCATE-GENERAL M. PHILLIPPE LEGER

18. The right of establishment and the provision of services constitute two separate branches of Community law, which are dealt with in two separate chapters of the EC Treaty and do not overlap.

19. The principle of freedom of establishment aims to foster the free movement of self-employed persons by enabling a self-employed person from one Member State to establish himself in another Member State on the same terms as a national of the latter State. In other words, "... establishment means integration into a national economy".

20. The principle of freedom to provide services merely enables a self-employed person established in a Member State in which he is integrated to exercise his activity in another Member State.

21. Establishment and the provision of services are mutually *exclusive*: it emerges clearly from Article 60 EC that the provisions on freedom to provide services are applicable only on condition that those on freedom of establishment are not applicable.

22. The rules governing those two major freedoms are very different. Thus, the activity of lawyers as providers of services is the subject of harmonising Directive 77/249, which enables services to be freely provided under the original professional qualification, whereas conditions for the establishment of lawyers have not—yet—been the subject of an actual harmonising directive. The establishment of lawyers is governed by Articles 52 et seq. of the Treaty...

> **Link**
> See the Lawyers Establishment Directive 98/5

He went on to spell out the problem and ways of resolving it:

86... [T]he distinction between the provision of services and establishment is not based on a single criterion ...

87. Consequently, there is a range of *indicia* which enables the provision of services to be distinguished from establishment.

88. The location of the lawyer's main centre of activity, the place where he has his principal residence, the size of his turnover in the various Member States in which he

carries out his activity, the amount of time spent in each of those States and the place at which he is entered on the Bar rolls will each afford evidence for the purpose of determining the nature of his activity in each of the Member States considered.

JUDGMENT

... [25] The concept of establishment within the meaning of the Treaty is ... a very broad one, allowing a Community national to participate, on a stable and continuous basis, in the economic life of a Member State other than his State of origin and to profit therefrom, so contributing to economic and social interpenetration within the Community in the sphere of activities as self-employed persons (see, to this effect, *Case 2/74, Reyners v. Belgium*).

[26] In contrast, where the provider of services moves to another Member State, the provisions of the chapter on services, in particular the third paragraph of Article 60, envisage that he is to pursue his activity there on a temporary basis.

[27] As the Advocate General has pointed out, the temporary nature of the activities in question has to be determined in the light, not only of the duration of the provision of the service, but also of its regularity, periodicity or continuity. The fact that the provision of services is temporary does not mean that the provider of services within the meaning of the Treaty may not equip himself with some form of infrastructure in the host Member State (including an office, chambers or consulting rooms) in so far as such infrastructure is necessary for the purposes of performing the services in question.

[28] However, that situation is to be distinguished from that of Mr Gebhard who, as a national of a Member State, pursues a professional activity on a stable and continuous basis in another Member State where he holds himself out from an established professional base to, amongst others, nationals of that State. Such a national comes under the provisions of the chapter relating to the right of establishment and not those of the chapter relating to services...

[35] However, the taking-up and pursuit of certain self-employed activities may be conditional on complying with certain provisions laid down by law, regulation or administrative action justified by the general good, such as rules relating to organisation, qualifications, professional ethics, supervision and liability (see *Case C-71/76, Thieffry v. Conseil de l'Ordre des Avocats À la Cour de Paris*). Such provisions may stipulate in particular that pursuit of a particular activity is restricted to holders of a diploma, certificate or other evidence of formal qualifications, to persons belonging to a professional body or to persons subject to particular rules or supervision, as the case may be. They may also lay down the conditions for the use of professional titles, such as *avvocato*.

Decipher

Note the four conditions are relevant to all of the fundamental freedoms rendering a common approach to the removal of obstacles across them all.

[37] It follows, however, from the Court's case law that national measures liable to hinder or make less attractive the exercise of fundamental freedoms guaranteed by the Treaty must fulfil four conditions: they must be applied in a non-discriminatory manner; they must be justified by imperative requirements in the general interest; they must be suitable for securing the attainment of the objective which they pursue; and they must

not go beyond what is necessary in order to attain it (see Case C-19/92, *Kraus v. Land Badenwürttemberg.*

[38] Likewise, in applying their national provisions, Member States may not ignore the knowledge and qualifications already acquired by the person concerned in another Member State (Case C-340/89, *Vlassopoulou v. Ministerium für Justiz, Bundesund Europaangelegenheiten Baden-Württemberg.* Consequently, they must take account of the equivalence of diplomas (see the judgment in *Thieffry* and, if necessary, proceed to a comparison of the knowledge and qualifications required by their national rules and those of the person concerned (see the judgment in *Vlassopoulou*).

There are many similarities between the Treaty freedoms and the approach taken to their interpretation by the ECJ. This was a case drawing a distinction, in this case between the Freedoms of Establishment and the Provision of Services. In doing so however it also pointed out the similarity of approach which the ECJ adopts when resolving obstacles across all of the fundamental freedoms.

While this case established the criteria to differentiate between the Freedoms of Establishment and Provision of Services the distinction between these is still a fine one. While the decision in *Gebhard* and similar cases such as *R v SS Transport exp Factortame Ltd (No 1)* Case 213/89 [1991] 3 CMLR 589 help to clarify such distinctions, cases brought before the ECJ will still often make reference to both of these freedoms, leaving any final decision to be made by the court.

J. Knoors v Secretary of State for Economic Affairs Case 115/78 [1979] 2 CMLR 357

Panel: Kutscher CJ, Mertens de Wilmars and Lord Mackenzie Stuart PPC, Donner, Pescatore, Sørensen, O'Keeffe, Bosco and Touffait JJHerr Gerhard Reischl, Advocate-General

Legislation: Arts 54 (ex Art 48), 49 (ex Art 43) and 56 (ex Art 49)

Facts: The plaintiff had trained in the Netherlands as an engine fitter but in 1963 married a Belgian national and settled with her at Dilsen in Belgium. He was employed at his father in laws plumbing and heating business before becoming an independent plumber in his own right in 1970. In 1976 he applied for requisite authority to work as a plumber in the Netherlands but was refused on the grounds that he lacked the requisite Dutch qualifications. He argued that he had worked as a plumber for 15 years in Belgium and ought to be treated as a Belgian plumber would, in accordance with the Treaty.

The Dutch authorities argued two points:

Firstly, that to allow him to do this would circumvent their national training requirements and create a precedent whereby tradesmen would simply train abroad to avoid the Dutch training requirements; and secondly, as a Dutch national he could not invoke the Treaty in his own state. He could not be a beneficiary of Treaty rights in such a situation.

ADVOCATE-GENERAL REISCHL

… It is simply absurd for the plaintiff to be treated differently from a Belgian or national of another member-State in the same situation solely because of his Dutch nationality. Such a procedure would be clear discrimination against the plaintiff exclusively on the ground of his nationality, which would be absolutely incompatible with the principles laid down in the EEC Treaty.

… He was and is therefore in the same situation as a Belgian national with the same background. The Commission correctly refers to the fact that if the interpretation put forward by the Dutch Government were followed the freedom of movement for all persons who have exercised their right to freedom of movement and have learned or carried on another occupation in the member-State in which they established themselves would in practice be restricted in so far as they would be unable to return to their home State without having to expect difficulties with regard to the exercise of their new occupation

JUDGMENT

[15] The General Programme for the abolition of restrictions on freedom to provide services, in the first indent of Title I, defines as beneficiaries the 'nationals of member-States who are established within the Community,' without making any distinction as to the nationality or residence of the persons concerned.

[16] The same idea is expressed by Title I of the General Programme for the abolition of restrictions on freedom of establishment, which designates as beneficiaries, in the first and third indents, the 'nationals of member-States' without any distinction as regards nationality or residence.

[17] It may therefore be stated that Directive 64/427 is based on a broad definition of the 'beneficiaries' of its provisions, in the sense that the nationals of all member-States must be able to avail themselves of the liberalising measures which it lays down, provided that they come objectively within one of the situations provided for by the directive, and no differentiation of treatment on the basis of their residence or nationality is permitted.

[18] Thus the provisions of the directive may be relied upon by the nationals of all the member-States who are in the situations which the directive defines for its application, even in respect of the State whose nationality they possess.

[19] This interpretation is justified by the requirements flowing from freedom of movement for persons, freedom of establishment and freedom to provide services, which are guaranteed by Articles 3(c), 48, 52 and 59 of the Treaty.

[20] In fact, these liberties, which are fundamental in the Community system, could not be fully realised if the member-States were in a position to refuse to grant the benefit of the provisions of Community law to those of their nationals who have taken advantage of the facilities existing in the matter of freedom of movement and who have acquired, by virtue of such facilities, the trade qualifications referred to by the directive in a member-State other than that whose nationality they possess…

[24] Although it is true that the provisions of the Treaty relating to establishment and the provision of services cannot be applied to situations which are purely internal to a member-State, the position nevertheless remains that the reference in Article 52 to 'nationals of a member-State' who wish to establish themselves 'in the territory of another member-State' cannot be interpreted in such a way as to exclude from the benefit of Community law a given member-State's own nationals when the latter, owing to the fact that they have lawfully resided on the territory of another member-State and have there acquired a trade qualification which is recognised by the provisions of Community law, are, with regard to their State of origin, in a situation which may be assimilated to that of any other persons enjoying the rights and liberties guaranteed by the Treaty.

[25] However, it is not possible to disregard the legitimate interest which a member-State may have in preventing certain of its nationals, by means of facilities created under the Treaty, from attempting wrongly to evade he application of their national legislation as regards training for a trade.

[26] In this case, however, it should be borne in mind that, having regard to the nature of the trades in question, the precise conditions set out in Article 3 of Directive 64/427, as regards the length of periods during which the activity in question must have been pursued, have the effect of excluding, in the fields in question, the risk of abuse referred to by the Dutch Government.

Note in paragraph 26 the basic premise of the ECJ's argument is that as long as there is an EU directive creating minimum qualifications for a particular trade or profession throughout all Member States (as there was here) then there is no risk to the EU in accepting migrants on the basis of the mutual recognition of qualifications.

Knoors case resolved what at first sight seemed a difficult issue: could Art 49 (ex Art 43) be applied internally within the EU citizen's home state? It spelt out that the need to make out a cross border element is crucial. Purely internal matters will not be subject to EU law. If an EU element existed then as long as there is no evidence of an abuse of EU rights by the individual (ie an attempt to circumvent minimum EU accepted professional or trade qualifications) then Art 49 must have application within the Member State.

Irene Vlassopoulou v Ministerium für Justiz, Bundes- und Europaangelegenheiten Baden-Württemberg (Ministry of Justice, Federal and European Affairs of the Province of Baden-Württemberg) Case 340/89 [1993] 2 CMLR 221

Panel: Due CJ, Rodríguez Iglesias and Díez de Velasco PPC, Slynn , Kakouris, Joliet, Grévisse, Zuleeg and Kapteyn JJ. Mr. Walter Van Gerven, Advocate-General

Legislation: Art 49 (ex Art 43)

Facts: In 1982 Mrs Irene Vlassopoulou, a Greek national, was both admitted to the Athens Bar and also submitted her doctoral thesis to the University of Tübingen (Germany). In July 1983 she began working in a firm of German lawyers in Mannheim and although practising in Greece, her main practice was in Mannheim dealing with Greek and EU law. As far was German law was concerned, Mrs Vlassopoulou practised under the responsibility of one of her German colleagues in the firm.

In 1988 her application to be admitted as a German lawyer was refused on the grounds that she did not possess the German professional education and training. Her appeal against this led to the Bundesgerichtshof (German appeal body) referring the following question to the ECJ for a preliminary ruling:

Is freedom of establishment within the meaning of Article 49 EEC infringed if a Community national who is already admitted and practising as a lawyer in her country of origin and for five years has been admitted in the host country as a legal adviser (Rechtsbeistand) and also practises in a law firm established there can be admitted as a lawyer in the host country only in accordance with the statutory rules of that country?

At an early part of its judgment the ECJ pointed out that where there has been no progress made by the Commission in the harmonising of professional qualifications then the Member States have the need to ensure the maintenance of professional standards.

JUDGMENT

... [9] In this regard, it must be stated first of all that in the absence of harmonisation of the conditions of access to a particular occupation the member-States are entitled to lay down the knowledge and qualifications needed in order to pursue it and to require the production of a diploma certifying that the holder has the relevant knowledge and qualifications: see Case 222/86, *Union Nationale des Entraineurs et Cadres Techniques Professionnels du Football (UNECTEF) v. Heylens.*

[14] Moreover, it is also clear from Case 71/76, *Thieffry v. Conseil de l'Ordre des Avocats À la Cour de Paris* that, in so far as Community law makes no special provision, the objectives of the Treaty, and in particular freedom of establishment, may be achieved by measures enacted by the member-States, which, under Article 5 EEC, must take 'all appropriate measures, whether general or particular, to ensure fulfilment of the obligations arising out of this Treaty or resulting from action taken by the institutions of the Community' and abstain from 'any measure which could jeopardise the attainment of the objectives of this Treaty.'

[15] It must be stated in this regard that, even if applied without any discrimination on the basis of nationality, national requirements concerning qualifications may have the effect of hindering nationals of the other member-States in the exercise of their right of establishment guaranteed to them by Article 52 EEC. That could be the case if the national rules in question took no account of the knowledge and qualifications already acquired by the person concerned in another member-State.

[16] Consequently, a member-State which receives a request to admit a person to a profession to which access, under national law, depends upon the possession of a diploma or a professional qualification must take into consideration the diplomas, certificates and other evidence of qualifications which the person concerned has

 Alert

acquired in order to exercise the same profession in another member-State by making a comparison between the specialised knowledge and abilities certified by those diplomas and the knowledge and qualifications required by the national rules.

[17] That examination procedure must enable the authorities of the host member-State to assure themselves, on an objective basis, that the foreign diploma certifies that its holder has knowledge and qualifications which are, if not identical, at least equivalent to those certified by the national diploma. That assessment of the equivalence of the foreign diploma must be carried out exclusively in the light of the level of knowledge and qualifications which its holder can be assumed to possess in the light of that diploma, having regard to the nature and duration of the studies and practical training to which the diploma relates: see Case 222/86, *UNECTEF v. Heylens*, cited above.

[18] In the course of that examination, a member-State may, however, take into consideration objective differences relating to both the legal framework of the profession in question in the member-State of origin and to its field of activity. In the case of the profession of lawyer, a member-State may therefore carry out a comparative examination of diplomas, taking account of the differences identified between the national legal systems concerned.

[19] If that comparative examination of diplomas results in the finding that the knowledge and qualifications certified by the foreign diploma correspond to those required by the national provisions, the member-State must recognise that diploma as fulfilling the requirements laid down by its national provisions. If, on the other hand, the comparison reveals that the knowledge and qualifications certified by the foreign diploma and those required by the national provisions correspond only partially, the host member-State is entitled to require the person concerned to show that he has acquired the knowledge and qualifications which are lacking.

Alert

[20] In this regard, the competent national authorities must assess whether the knowledge acquired in the host member-State, either during a course of study or by way of practical experience, is sufficient in order to prove possession of the knowledge which is lacking.

[21] If completion of a period of preparation or training for entry into the profession is required by the rules applying in the host member-State, those national authorities must determine whether professional experience acquired in the member-State of origin or in the host member-State may be regarded as satisfying that requirement in full or in part.

[22]... It follows that any decision taken must be capable of being made the subject of judicial proceedings in which its legality under Community law can be reviewed and that the person concerned must be able to ascertain the reasons for the decision taken in his regard: see Case 222/86, *UNECTEF v. Heylens*, cited above.

[23] Consequently, the answer to the question submitted by the Bundesgerichtshof must be that Article 52 EEC must be interpreted as requiring the national authorities of a member-State to which an application for admission to the profession of lawyer is made by a Community subject who is already admitted to practise as a lawyer in his country of origin and who practises as a legal adviser in the first-mentioned member-

State to examine to what extent the knowledge and qualifications attested by the diploma obtained by the person concerned in his country of origin correspond to those required by the rules of the host State; if those diplomas correspond only partially, the national authorities in question are entitled to require the person concerned to prove that he has acquired the knowledge and qualifications which are lacking.

The difficulty in balancing Member State concerns over adequate professional standards with the Treaty requirement of freedom of Establishment throughout the EU has already been seen in *Thieffry*. However *Vlassopoulou* is useful in collecting together in one case all of the requirements that ought to be followed by a Member State when it is assessing whether a migrant professional claiming Establishment under Art 49 possesses the appropriate skill and knowledge (in the absence of harmonising legislation). It is the basic formula in this case which was to be subsequently followed by the mutual recognition legislation itself.

Even today where there is no appropriate directive the case law will be used to require the State to take both the qualifications and appropriate experience into account. Of course where there is appropriate legislation then a Member State must follow this and ignore its own national standards.

The process of creating legislation began by attempting to harmonise the differing national standards across the EU but this was abandoned in the face of the endless problems involved. The solution was to be found by resolving the problem by a short progression of mutual recognition directives beginning with Directive 89/48 [1989] OJ L19/16. A 'residual directive' this was meant to cover all regulated professions requiring university level education of at least three years and not covered by a specific directive. It embraced the mutual recognition principle of *Vlassopoulou*. The approach is similar to the Dual Burden rule in the Free Movement of Goods; a professional in one Member State ought to be recognised as such in another.

Directive 89/48 was then supplemented by Directive 92/51 [1992] OJ L208/25 which covered courses other than three year higher education courses before both being amended by Directive 2001/19 [2001] OJ L206/1 (The SLIM directive) and then replaced by Directive 2005/36 OJ L255/22 covering both Establishment and Services.

Abdullah Tawil-Albertini v Ministre des Affaires Sociales Case 154/93 [1995] 1 CMLR 612

Panel: Due CJ, Díez de Velasco and Edward (rapporteur) PPC, Kakouris, Joliet, Schockweiler and Zuleeg JJ. M. Marco Darmon, Advocate-General

Legislation: Directives 78/686 and 78/687

Facts: Abdullah Tawil-Albertini, was a French national who had qualified as a dentist in the Lebanon. After Belgium recognised his Lebanese qualification as equivalent to their own, he was authorised to practise in Belgium. He was also authorised to practise in the UK and Ireland. However the French authorities refused to allow him to practise in France and upon his appeal the court referred the question of whether qualifications obtained by virtue of equivalence and which have not been acquired in one of the Member States of the EU could be covered by the mutual recognition principle.

JUDGMENT

[11] It should be noted that Article 2 of Directive 78/686 provides for the mutual recognition by Member States of qualifications in dentistry exhaustively listed in Article 3 and awarded by those States. That recognition has been automatic since the implementation of the directive because, concurrently, Directive 78/687 defined the minimum criteria which dental training in the various States of the Community must satisfy. The mutual recognition of qualifications in dentistry awarded by the Member States, mentioned in Directive 78/686, is based on the guarantees provided by the application of minimum criteria for training imposed by Directive 78/687.

[12] In relations with non-member States, such co-ordination of legislation on training can be established only by agreements concluded between the States concerned. Thus, by virtue of Article 1(4) of Directive 78/687, Member States remain free, in accordance with their own rules in respect of their own territory, to authorise holders of qualifications obtained in non-Community States to take up and pursue the activities of a dental practitioner.

[13] Accordingly, recognition by a Member State of qualifications awarded by non-member States does not bind the other Member States.

[14] Article 7 concerns only qualifications awarded by the Member States.

[15] The answer to the question referred to the Court for a preliminary ruling should therefore be that Article 7 of Directive 78/686 does not require Member States to recognise diplomas, certificates and other evidence of formal qualifications which do not testify to dental training acquired in one of the Member States of the Community.

Alert

Unlike the other cases in this chapter this is a case decided after the implementation of EU legislation. The legislation in question, Directive 78/686 allowed for the mutual recognition of dental qualifications across the EU. This case sought a more detailed answer as to what was meant by mutual recognition and how far mutual recognition could be taken. If one Member State has acknowledged a non EU qualification as equivalent to its own national standard then must other Member States do likewise?

In answering this question the court pointed out that the only reason mutual recognition works is because the EU directives guarantee minimum standards of professional competence across the EU. Individual Member States were free to establish similar arrangements with non-EU states but only on an individual basis. This could not oblige other Member States to do likewise. If such a state were to grant recognition to the qualification, however, they would have to take any period of professional experience gained in another Member State into account when assessing any shortfall in professional competence.

Note that in this case Tawil Albertini was an EU citizen by reason of his French nationality. This case could not have been brought otherwise.

Centros Ltd v Erhvervs- og Selskabsstyrelsen Case C-212/97 [1999] 2 CMLR 551

Panel: Rodríguez Iglesias P, Kapteyn, Puissochet, Hirsch and Jann PPC, Mancini, Moitinho de Almeid, Gulmann, Murray, Edward, Ragnemalm, Sevón, Wathelet (Rapporteur), Schintgen and Ioannou JJ. Mr Antonio La Pergola, Advocate-General

Legislation: Art 49 (ex Art 43), Art 61 (ex Art 54) and Art 54 (ex Art 48)

Facts: Centros was a private limited company registered in England and Wales. Mr and Mrs Bryde were business partners with Mrs Bryde being the sole registered director of Centros Ltd. They were both Danish nationals residing in Denmark. They bought Centros Ltd intending it to be a wine import and export business. Its company address was that of a personal friend in the UK. They applied to the Danish authorities to register a branch of Centros in Denmark. Danish law did not impose any requirement as to minimum capital for companies from other EU countries seeking to establish a branch in Danish territory. However Danish law did require a substantial minimum paid up share capital to incorporate a company in Denmark. This sum was intended to be used as a reserve to pay creditors in the event of a bankruptcy. By only registering a branch in Denmark the Brydes hoped to avoid this sum. For this reason the Danish authorities turned down their application arguing that they were protecting creditors by preventing fraudulent insolvencies.

The national court referred to the ECJ the question whether it was compatible with Art 49 to refuse registration of a branch of a company which had its registered office in another Member State yet intended to carry out its entire business in the country in which the branch was established in order to avoid paying company capital?

JUDGMENT

[24] It is true that according to the case law of the Court a Member State is entitled to take measures designed to prevent certain of its nationals from attempting, under cover of the rights created by the Treaty, improperly to circumvent their national legislation or to prevent individuals from improperly or fraudulently taking advantage of provisions of Community law.

[25] However, although, in such circumstances, the national courts may, case by case, take account—on the basis of objective evidence—of abuse or fraudulent conduct on the part of the persons concerned in order, where appropriate, to deny them the benefit of the provisions of Community law on which they seek to rely, they must nevertheless assess such conduct in the light of the objectives pursued by those provisions.

[26] In the present case, the provisions of national law, application of which the parties concerned have sought to avoid, are rules governing the formation of companies and not rules concerning the carrying on of certain trades, professions or businesses. The provisions of the Treaty on freedom of establishment are intended specifically to enable companies formed in accordance with the law of a Member State and having their registered office, central administration or principal place of business within the

Community to pursue activities in other Member States though an agency, branch or subsidiary.

[27] That being so, the fact that a national of a Member State who wishes to set up a company chooses to form it in the Member State whose rules of company law seem to him the least restrictive and to set up branches in other Member States cannot, in itself, constitute an abuse of the right of establishment. The right to form a company in accordance with the law of a Member State and to set up branches in other Member States is inherent in the exercise, in a single market, of the freedom of establishment guaranteed by the Treaty.

[28] In this connection, the fact that company law is not completely harmonised in the Community is of little consequence. Moreover, it is always open to the Council, on the basis of the powers conferred upon it by Article 54(3)(g) E.C. , to achieve complete harmonisation.

[29] In addition, it is clear from paragraph [16] of *Segers* that the fact that a company does not conduct any business in the Member State in which it has its registered office and pursues its activities only in the Member State where its branch is established is not sufficient to prove the existence of abuse or fraudulent conduct which would entitle the latter Member State to deny that company the benefit of the provisions of Community law relating to the right of establishment.

[30] Accordingly, the refusal of a Member State to register a branch of a company formed in accordance with the law of another Member State in which it has its registered office on the grounds that the branch is intended to enable the company to carry on all its economic activity in the host State, with the result that the secondary establishment escapes national rules on the provision for and the paying-up of a minimum capital, is incompatible with Articles 52 and 58, in so far as it prevents any exercise of the right freely to set up a secondary establishment which Articles 52 and 58 are specifically intended to guarantee.

Alert

Article 49 is unusual amongst some of the other Free Movement provisions in that it also applies to companies as well as natural persons. However the basic principles which have been seen to apply in earlier case law are equally relevant here. Art 54 in fact specifies that companies or firms '… be treated in the same way as natural persons who are nationals of Member States.'

2 Freedom to Provide Services

Procureur du Roi v Marc Debauve and Others; S.A. Compagnie Generale pour la Diffusion de la Television; Coditel and Others v S.A. Cine Vog Films and Others **Case 52/79 [1981] 2 CMLR 362**

Panel: Kutscher CJ, O'Keeffe and Touffait PPC, Mertens de Wilmars, Pescatore, Lord Mackenzie Stuart, Bosco, Koopmans and Due JJ. Mr. Jean-Pierre Warner, Advocate-General

Legislation: Art 56 (ex Art 49) and Art 57 (ex Art 50)

Facts: Cable broadcasting companies operating within Belgium were prosecuted by the Belgian authorities for allowing the broadcasting of advertisements during their programmes contrary to Belgian law of that time. The main company that we are concerned with in this case would receive aerial television signals that had been broadcast over the air and then distribute these by cable to the television sets of their subscribers; such cable diffusion had a number of advantages for the subscribers to this service. Such subscribers received all TV programmes through the cable including both Belgian and foreign but it was the foreign broadcasts which contained the advertisements and which breached Belgian law. The effect of Belgian law upon the cable companies was to require them to blot out any advertisements in foreign programmes that they relayed. The principle question addressed by way of preliminary reference to the ECJ was whether the Belgian law prohibiting the transmission of adverts interfered with the right to receive a broadcasting service even though it was possible to receive these adverts in those parts of Belgium within the natural zone of broadcasting from the foreign stations? While the Belgian measure was only indirectly discriminatory did it have a disproportionate effect?

In its findings the court very quickly arrived at the main issue of this case:

JUDGMENT

... [9] However, it should be observed that the provisions of the Treaty on freedom to provide services cannot apply to activities whose relevant elements are confined within a single member-State. Whether that is the case depends on findings of fact which are for the national court to establish. Since the Tribunal Correctionnel has concluded that in the given circumstances of this case the services out of which the prosecutions brought before it arose are such as to come under provisions of the Treaty relating to services, the questions referred to the Court should be examined from the same point of view.

[10] The central question raised by the national court is whether Articles 59 and 60 of the Treaty must be interpreted as prohibiting all national rules against the transmission of advertisements by cable television to the extent to which such rules do not make any distinction based on the origin of the advertisements, the nationality of the person providing the services or his place of establishment.

[11] According to the first paragraph of Article 59 of the Treaty restrictions on freedom to provide services within the Community shall be progressively abolished during the transitional period in respect of nationals of member-States of the Community. The strict requirements of that provision involve the abolition of all discrimination against a provider of services on the grounds of his nationality or of the fact that he is established in a member-State other than that where the service is to be provided.

[12] In view of the particular nature of certain services such as the broadcasting and transmission of television signals, specific requirements imposed upon providers of services which are founded upon the application of rules regulating certain types of activity and which are justified by the general interest and apply to all persons and

undertakings established within the territory of the said member-State cannot be said to be incompatible with the Treaty to the extent to which a provider of services established in another member-State is not subject to similar regulations there.

[13] From information given to the Court during these proceedings it appears that the television broadcasting of advertisements is subject to widely divergent systems of law in the various member-States, passing from almost total prohibition, as in Belgium, by way of rules comprising more or less strict restrictions, to systems affording broad commercial freedom. In the absence of any approximation of national laws and taking into account the considerations of general interest underlying the restrictive rules in this area, the application of the laws in question cannot be regarded as a restriction upon freedom to provide services so long as those laws treat all such services identically whatever their origin or the nationality or place of establishment of the persons providing them.

Alert

[14] A prohibition of the type contained in the Belgian legislation referred to by the national court should be judged in the light of those considerations. It must be stressed that the prohibition on the transmission of advertisements by cable television contained in the Royal Decree referred to above cannot be examined in isolation. A review of all the Belgian legislation on broadcasting shows that that prohibition is the corollary of the ban on the broadcasting of commercial advertisements imposed on the Belgian broadcasting organisations. This is also the way in which the judgment making the reference sets out the relevant legislation, indicating that the Royal Decree prohibits the transmission of advertisements in order to maintain conformity with the scheme imposed on the national broadcasting organisations.

[15] In the absence of any harmonization of the relevant rules, a prohibition of this type falls within the residual power of each member-State to regulate, restrict or even totally prohibit television advertising on its territory on grounds of general interest. The position is not altered by the fact that such restrictions or prohibitions extend to television advertising originating in other member-States in so far as they are actually applied on the same terms to national television organisations.

[16] The answer must therefore be that Articles 59 and 60 of the Treaty do not preclude national rules prohibiting the transmission of advertisements by cable television—as they prohibit the broadcasting of advertisements by television—if those rules are applied without distinction as regards the origin, whether national or foreign, of those advertisements, the nationality of the person providing the service, or the place where he is established.

[17] In view of that answer the question concerning the consequences which may arise from the direct applicability of Articles 59 and 60 of the Treaty where there is conflict between those provisions and national legislation has become devoid of object.

Further illustrations in which a cross border element was decided upon the individual facts of the case can be seen in *Christelle Deliege v Lingua Francophone de Judo et Disciplines Associees* Cases 51/96 and 191/97 [2002] 2 CMLR 65 in which the contestant took part in competitions in other Member states or *Francoise De Coster v*

College des Bourgmestres et Echevins de Watermael-Boitsford Case 17/00 [2002] 1 CMLR 285 where a tax on the ownership of satellite dishes could only interfere with the reception of foreign broadcasting services.

Society for the Protection of Unborn Children Ireland Ltd. (S.P.U.C.) v Stephen Grogan and Others (Case C-159/90) [1991] 3 CMLR 849

Panel: Presiding, Due CJ, Mancini, O'Higgins, Moitinho de Almeida, Rodríguez Iglesias and Díez de Velasco PPC, Slynn, Kakouris Joliet, Schockweiler, Grévisse, Zuleeg and Kapteyn JJ. Mr. Walter Van Gerven, Advocate-General

Legislation: Art 57 (ex Art 50), Art 56 (ex Art 49) and Art 60 (ex Art 53)

Facts: Abortions were illegal in Eire and the Society for the Protection of Unborn Children Ireland Ltd. ('SPUC') was a company incorporated in Eire to prevent the decriminalisation of abortion in that country. It brought a case in the Irish High Court seeking an injunction against Stephen Grogan and fourteen other officers of students associations to prevent their distributing information to students concerning the location of clinics in the UK where abortions were carried out. The student organisations concerned had no links with the particular clinics mentioned.

The first two questions referred to the ECJ by the High Court for a preliminary ruling asked:

(a) Does carrying out an abortion come within the definition of 'services' provided for in Art 60?

(b) Can a Member State prohibit the distribution of specific information about the identity, location and means of communication with a specified clinic or clinics in another Member State where abortions are performed?

JUDGMENT

[16] In its first question, the national court essentially seeks to establish whether medical termination of pregnancy, performed in accordance with the law of the State where it is carried out, constitutes a service within the meaning of Article 60 EEC.

[17] According to the first paragraph of that provision, services are to be considered to be 'services' within the meaning of the Treaty where they are normally provided for remuneration, in so far as they are not governed by the provisions relating to freedom of movement for goods, capital or persons. Indent (d) of the second paragraph of Article 60 expressly states that activities of the professions fall within the definition of services.

[18] It must be held that termination of pregnancy, as lawfully practised in several member-States, is a medical activity which is normally provided for remuneration and may be carried out as part of a professional activity. In any event, the Court has already held in *Luisi* and *Carbone* that medical activities fall within the scope of Article 60 EEC.

[22] Having regard to the facts of the case, it must be considered that, in its second... question, the national court seeks essentially to establish whether it is contrary to

Community law for a member-State in which medical termination of pregnancy is forbidden to prohibit students associations from distributing information about the identity and location of clinics in another member-State where voluntary termination of pregnancy is lawfully carried out and the means of communicating with those clinics, where the clinics in question have no involvement in the distribution of the said information.

[23] Although the national court's questions refer to Community law in general, the Court takes the view that its attention should be focused on the provisions of Article 59 *et seq.* EEC, which deal with the freedom to provide services...

[24] As regards, first, the provisions of Article 59 EEC, which prohibit any restriction on the freedom to supply services, it is apparent from the facts of the case that the link between the activity of the students associations of which Mr. Grogan and the other defendants are officers and medical terminations of pregnancies carried out in clinics in another member-State is too tenuous for the prohibition on the distribution of information to be capable of being regarded as a restriction within the meaning of Article 59.

[25] The situation in which students associations distributing the information at issue in the main proceedings are not in co-operation with the clinics whose addresses they publish can be distinguished from the situation which gave rise to the judgment in GB-INNO-BM, in which the Court held that a prohibition on the distribution of advertising was capable of constituting a barrier to the free movement of goods and therefore had to be examined in the light of Articles 30, 31 and 36 EEC.

[26] The information to which the national court's questions refer is not distributed on behalf of an economic operator established in another member-State. On the contrary, the information constitutes a manifestation of freedom of expression and of the freedom to impart and receive information which is independent of the economic activity carried on by clinics established in another member-State.

[27] It follows that, in any event, a prohibition on the distribution of information in circumstances such as those which are the subject of the main proceedings cannot be regarded as a restriction within the meaning of EEC ...

[32] The reply to the national court's second and third questions must therefore be that it is not contrary to Community law for a member-State in which medical termination of pregnancy is forbidden to prohibit students associations from distributing information about the identity and location of clinics in another member-State where voluntary termination of pregnancy is lawfully carried out and the means of communicating with those clinics, where the clinics in question have no involvement in the distribution of the said information.

The distinction between the Freedom of Establishment and the Freedom to Provide Services has already been examined in this chapter under the case of *Gebhard*. *Grogan* was a seminal case in revealing the extent of what could be seen as a service and hence fall under Art 56.

Note that at the time of this case a great many Irish women travelled to the UK to obtain abortions. The students' organisations concerned were challenging the whole matter as not simply as aspect of the provision of services but as part of a wider issue of human rights.

Ultimately the court was able to avoid the thorny abortion issue by distinguishing between the provision of abortions as a service for remuneration and the distribution of information about such abortion clinics which was not being provided for remuneration. Had such information been provided on behalf of the clinics it would have been seen as a service and fallen under the protection of Arts 49 and 50.

The issue of what amounts to remuneration would be discussed again in *Deliege v Ligue Francophone de Judo et Disciplines Associees Asbl and Others* (Joined Cases 51/96 and 191/97) [2002] 2 CMLR 65 where judo would be seen as an economic activity capable of being subject to remuneration even though the remuneration was provided by sponsors and similar outside bodies rather than as a result of a normal employment contract.

Graziana Luisi and Giuseppe Carbone v Ministero del Tesoro Cases 286/82 & 26/83 [1985] 3 CMLR 52

Panel: Presiding, Mertens de Wilmars CJ, Koopmans, Bahlmann and Galmot PPC, Pescatore, Lord Mackenzie Stuart, Bosco, Everling and Kakouris JJ. Sig. Federico Mancini, Advocate-General

Legislation: Art 57 (ex Art 50) and Art 59 (ex Art 52)

Case Facts: Two Italian residents, Mrs Graziana Luisi and Mr Giuseppe Carbone, were each fined by the Italian Minister for the Treasury for exceeding the limits on Italian currency which could be taken abroad at that time. The plaintiffs contested this decision on the basis that it was in breach of EU law. Mrs Luisi stated that she had used the money for reasons of tourism and medical treatment. Mr Carbone stated that he had used the money during as a tourist. Both plaintiffs argued that the restrictions on export of the means of payment for tourism or medical treatment were contrary to the provisions of the EU Treaty relating to current payments and the movement of capital. The main question for our purpose was whether the Italian limits on currency export were an impediment to the provision of services abroad.

ADVOCATE GENERAL SIG FEDERICO MANCINI

Let us begin with tourism ... A State which is free to limit or prohibit the export of foreign currency by its own residents is also free to deny them tourist services available in other member countries and thereby adversely to affect the business of whoever offers such services. ... Among the values embodied in the Treaty, the free movement of services stands in the forefront. To remove from it an extremely important economic sector such as tourism would be to curtail its scope drastically, ...

And the same may be said of health or educational facilities. To ask that the person moving from one country to another should be the doctor, who relies upon sophisticated instruments close at hand or operates only in a clinic where he has the necessary equipment and expert helpers, or to ask that it should be the school which goes to the place where the pupils reside, is unreasonable. ...

JUDGMENT

[9] According to Article 60 of the Treaty, services are deemed to be 'services' within the meaning of the Treaty where they are normally provided for remuneration, in so far as they are not governed by the provisions relating to freedom of movement for goods, capital and persons...

[10] By virtue of Article 59 of the Treaty, restrictions on freedom to provide such services are to be abolished in respect of nationals of member-States who are established in a member-State other than that of the person for whom the service is intended. In order to enable services to be provided, the person providing the service may go to the member-State where the person for whom it is provided is established or else the latter may go to the State in which the person providing the service is established. Whilst the former case is expressly mentioned in the third paragraph of Article 60, which permits the person providing the service to pursue his activity temporarily in the member-State where the service is provided, the latter case is the necessary corollary thereof, which fulfils the objective of liberalising all gainful activity not covered by the free movement of goods, persons and capital.

... 16] It follows that the freedom to provide services includes the freedom, for the recipients of services, to go to another member-State in order to receive a service there, without being obstructed by restrictions, even in relation to payments, and that tourists, persons receiving medical treatment and persons travelling for the purpose of education or business are to be regarded as recipients of services.

Alert

Article 49 specifically covers the removal of 'restrictions on freedom to provide services within the Community'. This case is seminal in establishing the breadth of application of Art 49 beyond the literal interpretation of its wording.

In extending the provision of services to the recipient *Luisi and Carbone* set a precedent that would lead logically enough to additional rights being acquired by the service recipient including education, health care and other public services. As in so many other areas the case law developed an approach which would essentially be followed by legislation eg the Services Directive (2006/123/EC).

Conclusion

The case law developing Freedom of Establishment and Provision of Services has followed the well worn path shared with the other Freedom provisions. The process normally begins with the removal of direct discrimination, then indirect discrimination before going on to delineate the extent of that particular freedom. The essential problem in all of these situations is the balancing of State and EU interests. While in this Chapter this has specifically been concerned with achieving a balance between the Member States legitimate concerns about the maintenance of professional standards and the EU need to establish a Europe wide availability for the services provided by professionals, common solutions with the other Freedoms will have been observed.

EU legislation however now plays a dominating part in achieving a broad measure of harmonisation and it is the interplay between legislation and case law that represents the most significant recent development.

Further Reading

Cabral, Pedro: 'The Internal Market and the Right to Cross Border Medical Care' (2004) 29 ELR 673

Fairhurst, John: *The Law of the European Union* 7th ed Longman/Peason Chapter 13

Horspool and Humphreys: *European Union Law* 4TH ed, OUP, Chapters 7 and 8

Siemms, Mathias: 'Convergance, Competition, Centros and Conflicts of law' (2002) 27 ELR 47

Steiner, Woods and Twigg-Flesner: *EU Law* 10th ed OUP Chapters 22,23 and 24

Free Movement of Workers

Alex Lawson

Introduction

This Chapter deals with the free movement of workers which is one of the central elements of the new legal order created by the Treaties and secondary legislation. It is regularly in the news headlines and is of huge significance, providing EU citizens with a range of important rights and privileges. The European Union has successfully created the largest (in terms of numbers of states) area without borders in the world today and probably in all human history.

1 Defining an 'Employment Relationship'

Deborah Lawrie-Blum v Land Baden-Württemberg Case 66/85 [1987] 3 CMLR 389

Panel: Lord Mackenzie Stuart CJ, Koopmans, Everling and Bahlmann PPC, Bosco, Due and Schockweiler JJ. Herr Carl Otto Lenz, Advocate-General

Legislation: Article 45 (ex Art 39, ex Art 48)

Facts: The applicant was a British national who attended the University of Freiburg to train to be a teacher. The German authorities claimed she was not a worker because, although paid for a few hours teaching each week, she was in reality training. This raised the question of how much work an individual had to undertake to qualify as a worker, particularly in a context in which they were clearly carrying out some other activity within the host state.

JUDGMENT

On the meaning of 'worker' in Article 48(1)

[12] Mrs. Lawrie-Blum considers that any paid activity must be regarded as an economic activity and that the sphere in which it is exercised must necessarily be of an economic nature. A restrictive interpretation of Article 48(1) would reduce freedom of movement to a mere instrument of economic integration, would be contrary to its broader objective of creating an area in which Community citizens enjoy freedom of movement and would deprive the exception in Article 48(4) of any meaning of its own. The term 'worker' covers any person performing for remuneration work the nature of which is not determined by himself for and under the control of another, regardless of the legal nature of the employment relationship.

[13] The Land Baden-Württemberg espouses the considerations put forward by the Bundesverwaltungsgericht in its order for reference to the effect that, since a trainee teacher's activity falls under education policy, it is not an economic activity within the meaning of Article 2 of the Treaty. The term 'worker' within the meaning of Article 48 of the Treaty and Regulation 1612/68 covers only persons whose relationship to their employer is governed by a contract subject to private law and not persons whose employment relationship is subject to public law. The period of preparatory service should be regarded as the last stage of the professional training of future teachers.

[14] The United Kingdom considers that a distinction between students and workers must be made on the basis of objective criteria and that the term 'worker' in Article 48 must be given a Community definition. Objectively defined, a 'worker' is a person who is obliged to provide services to another in return for monetary reward and who is subject to the direction or control of the other person as regards the way in which the work is done. In the present case, account must be taken of the fact that a trainee teacher is required, at least towards the end of the period of preparatory service, to conduct lessons and therefore provides an economically valuable service for which he receives remuneration which is based on the starting salary of a duly appointed teacher.

[15] The Commission takes the view that the criterion for the application of Article 48 is the existence of an employment relationship, regardless of the legal nature of that relationship and its purpose. The fact that the period of preparatory service is a compulsory stage in the preparation for the practice of a profession and that it is spent in the public service is irrelevant if the objective criteria for defining the term 'worker', namely the existence of a relationship of subordination vis-à-vis the employer, irrespective of the nature of that relationship, the actual provision of services and the payment of remuneration, are satisfied.

[16] Since freedom of movement for workers constitutes one of the fundamental principles of the Community, the term 'worker' in Article 48 may not be interpreted differently according to the law of each member-State but has a Community meaning. Since it defines the scope of that fundamental freedom, the Community concept of a 'worker' must be interpreted broadly Case 53/81 *Levin v. Staatssecretaris Van Justitie*.

[17] That concept must be defined in accordance with objective criteria which distinguish the employment relationship by reference to the rights and duties of the persons concerned. The essential feature of an employment relationship, however, is that for a certain period of time a person performs services for and under the direction of another person in return for which he receives remuneration.

Alert

[18] In the present case, it is clear that during the entire period of preparatory service the trainee teacher is under the direction and supervision of the school to which he is assigned. It is the school that determines the services to be performed by him and his working hours and it is the school's instructions that he must carry out and its rules that he must observe. During a substantial part of the preparatory service he is required to give lessons to the school's pupils and thus provides a service of some economic value to the school. The amounts which he receives may be regarded as remuneration for the services provided and for the duties involved in completing the period of preparatory service. Consequently, the three criteria for the existence of an employment relationship are fulfilled in this case.

[19] The fact that teachers' preparatory service, like apprenticeships in other occupations, may be regarded as practical preparation directly related to the actual pursuit of the occupation in point is not a bar to the application of Article 48(1) if the service is performed under the conditions of an activity as an employed person.

[20] Nor may it be objected that services performed in education do not fall within the scope of the EEC Treaty because they are not of an economic nature. All that is required for the application of Article 48 is that the activity should be in the nature of work performed for remuneration, irrespective of the sphere in which it is carried out (Case 36/74 *Walrave v. Union Cycliste Internationale*). Nor may the economic nature of those activities be denied on the ground that they are performed by persons whose status is governed by public law since, as the Court pointed out in its judgment in Case 152/73 (*Sotgiu v. Deutsche Bundespost*), the nature of the legal relationship between employee and employer, whether involving public law status or a private law contract, is immaterial as regards the application of Article 48 .

[21] The fact that trainee teachers give lessons for only a few hours a week and are paid remuneration below the starting salary of a qualified teacher does not prevent them from being regarded as workers. In its judgment in *Levin*, cited above, the Court held that the expressions 'worker' and 'activity as an employed person' must be understood as including persons who, because they are not employed full time, receive pay lower than that for full-time employment, provided that the activities performed are effective and genuine. The latter requirement is not called into question in this case.

Alert

[22] Consequently, the reply to the first part of the question must be that a trainee teacher who, under the direction and supervision of the school authorities, is undergoing a period of service in preparation for the teaching profession during which he provides services by giving lessons and receives remuneration must be regarded as a worker within the meaning of Article 48(1) EEC, irrespective of the legal nature of the employment relationship. ...

2   Is the Individual Pursuing an 'Effective and Genuine Activity'?

A worker for the purposes of Art 45 is defined as a person who is pursuing an 'effective and genuine activity'. This seeks to exclude people who are only carrying out marginal activity (i.e. of very little genuine economic significance). It should be noted that the ECJ has been reluctant to categorise activity in this way.

Levin v Staatssecretaris van Justitie Case 53/81 [1982] 2 CMLR 454

Panel: Mertens de Wilmars CJ, Bosco, Touffait and Due PPC, Pescatore, Lord Mackenzie Stuart, O'Keeffe, Koopmans, Everling, Chloros and Grévisse JJ. Sir Gordon Slynn, Advocate-General

Legislation: Regulation 1612/68

Facts: the applicant was a British national who had been refused a residence permit in the Netherlands on the basis that she was not working at the time of application. She argued that she had in fact begun part-time employment and, in any event, she and her husband (who was not an EU national) had sufficient resources to maintain themselves even without working. The applicant could thus be distinguished from other cases in that they were only a part time worker. The question for the ECJ was what level of activity was sufficient for an individual to be classified as a worker.

JUDGMENT

[10] The Dutch and Danish Governments have each argued that only persons whose wages are at least equal to the subsistence level regarded as necessary by the laws of the member-State where they work, or who work at least as many hours as is considered normal for full-time work in the sector concerned, can rely upon Article 48 of the EEC Treaty. Since Community legislation contains no provisions on the matter, recourse must be had, they say, to national criteria in order to determine both the minimum wage and the minimum number of hours.

[11] This argument cannot, however, be accepted. As the Court has already declared in its judgment of 19 March 1964, the terms 'worker' and 'work in paid employment' cannot be determined by reference to the legislation of the member-States, but have a meaning in Community law. Otherwise, the Community rules relating to the free movement of workers would be deprived of their effect, because the meaning of these terms could be fixed and varied unilaterally, outside the control of the Community institutions, by the national legislators, who could thus at will exclude particular categories of person from the application of the Treaty.

[12] This would particularly be the case if enjoyment of the rights accorded on the basis of the free movement of workers could be made dependent on a wage which the law of the host State regards as the minimum; because of this, the personal area of application of the Community rules on this subject could vary from member-State to member-State. The meaning and scope of the terms 'worker' and 'work in paid employment' must therefore be clarified in the light of the principles of the Community legal order.

[13] It must be emphasised in this connection that these terms determine the area of application of one of the fundamental freedoms guaranteed by the Treaty and must on this basis not be interpreted restrictively.

[14] In accordance with this view, the recitals to Regulation 1612/68 confirm in general terms the right of all workers of the member-States to do the work of their choice within the Community, regardless of whether they are permanent workers, seasonal workers or frontier workers, or workers who are employed in the framework of a supply of services. Moreover, while, by its Article 4, Directive 68/360 grants workers—on production of the document on which they have entered the territory, and of a confirmation of engagement or employment made by the employer—the right of residence, it does not make this right dependent on any condition as to the sort of work or the income earned thereby.

[15] An interpretation which accords to these terms their full scope is equally in keeping with the objectives of the Treaty, which, under Articles 2 and 3, includes the removal between the member-States of obstacles to the free movement of persons, *inter alia*, in order to promote the harmonious development of economic activity within the whole Community and to improve the standard of living. Since part-time work, although

possibly producing less income than that which is regarded as the minimum for subsistence, is for many an effective means of improving their living conditions, the beneficial effect of Community law would be undermined and the achievement of the objectives of the Treaty jeopardised if enjoyment of the rights accorded on the basis of the free movement of workers were reserved to persons who earn by full-time work wages which are at least equal to the minimum wage guaranteed in the sector concerned.

[16] Consequently, the terms 'worker' and 'work in paid employment' must be understood as meaning that the provisions relating to the free movement of workers also relate to persons who only perform or wish to perform part-time work in paid employment and who only receive or would only receive therefore a wage which is lower than the minimum wage guaranteed in the sector concerned. No distinction must be made here between those who are prepared to make do with their income from such work and those who supplement this income with other income, either from private resources or from the earnings of an accompanying member of their family.

Alert

[17] It must, however, be observed that, although part-time work does not fall outside the area of application of the provisions relating to the free movement of workers, these provisions only apply to the performance of real and actual work, to the exclusion of work of such small degree that it appears merely minimal and subsidiary. From the formulation of the principle of the free movement of persons and from the place occupied by the provisions relating to this matter in the overall system of the Treaty, it is clear that these provisions only guarantee free movement to persons who perform or wish to perform an activity of an economic nature.

[18] It must therefore be said in answer to the first and second questions that the provisions of Community law relating to the free movement of workers also apply to a citizen of a member-State who, on the territory of another member-State, works in paid employment which produces less income than is regarded in the latter member-State as the minimum for subsistence, regardless of whether the person concerned augments his income from such work in paid employment up to that minimum with other income or makes do with means of subsistence below the minimum, so long as he performs real and actual work in paid employment.

The third question

[19] The third question seeks in essence to know whether the right of entry to and residence in the territory of a member-State can be denied to a worker who, by his entry or residence, is pursuing principally other aims than the work in paid employment, as defined in the answer to the first and second questions.

[20] According to the wording of Article 48 (3) of the EEC Treaty, workers have the right to move freely within the territory of the member-States 'for the purpose' of accepting an offer of employment actually made. Under the same provision, they are entitled to remain in one of the member-States 'for the purpose' of carrying out an employed activity there. Moreover, the recitals to Regulation 1612/68 specify that free movement means the right for workers to move freely within the Community 'in order' to work there in paid employment, while, under Article 2 of Directive 68/360, the

member-States are obliged to allow workers to leave their territory 'in order' to accept or to perform work in paid employment on the territory of another member-State.

[21] From these formulations, however, there emerges only the requirement, inherent in the very principle of the free movement of workers, that the advantages accorded by Community law on the basis of this freedom can only be invoked by persons who are actually working in paid employment or who seriously wish to do so. These formulations, however, do not imply that enjoyment of this freedom can be made dependent on the motives of a citizen of a member-State in applying for entry to or residence on the territory of a member-State, so long as he performs or wishes to perform work which satisfies the above-mentioned criteria, that is to say, real and actual work in paid employment.

[22] Once this condition is satisfied, the worker's intentions in seeking work in the member-State concerned are irrelevant and must not be taken into account.

[23] It must therefore be said in answer to the third question posed by the Raad van State that any motives with which a worker from a member-State seeks work in another member-State are irrelevant to his right of entry to and residence on the territory of the latter State, so long as he performs or wishes to perform real and actual work in paid employment there. ...

Alert

Anita Groener v Minister for Education and City of Dublin Vocational Education Committee **Case 379/87 [1990] 1 CMLR 401**

Panel: Due CJ, Slynn, Kakouris, Schockweiler and Zuleeg PPC, Koopmans, Mancini, Joliet, O'Higgins, Moitinho de Almeida and Grevisse JJ. M. Marco Darmon, Advocate-General

Legislation: Regulation 1612/68

Facts: Groener was a Dutch art teacher who was refused an appointment as a lecturer in an Irish vocational school because she did not speak Irish (Gaeilge). This was not strictly a requirement of the job since the teaching of art in those schools was conducted in English. It was instead intended to assist in promoting the language as an aspect of government cultural policy. The ECJ held that the requirement did indirectly discriminate (not many non-Irish workers spoke Irish), but that the language requirement was not disproportionate to the policy objective and, therefore, was compatible with Reg 1612/68.

JUDGMENT

[14] Since the second indent of Article 3(1) is not applicable where linguistic requirements are justified by the nature of the post, it is appropriate to consider first the second question submitted by the national court, which is essentially whether the nature of a permanent full-time post of lecturer in art in public vocational education institutions is such as to justify the requirement of a knowledge of the Irish language.

[15] According to the documents before the Court, the teaching of art, like that of most other subjects taught in public vocational education schools, is conducted essentially or indeed exclusively in the English language. It follows that, as indicated by the terms of the second question submitted, knowledge of the Irish language is not required for the performance of the duties which teaching of the kind at issue specifically entails.

[16] However, that finding is not in itself sufficient to enable the national court to decide whether the linguistic requirement in question is justified 'by reason of the nature of the post to be filled' , within the

414 meaning of the last subparagraph of Article 3(1) of Regulation 1612/68.

[17] To apprehend the full scope of the second question, regard must be had to the special linguistic situation in Ireland, as it appears from the documents before the Court. By virtue of Article 8 of the Bunreacht na hEireann (Irish Constitution)

1. The Irish language as the national language is the first official language.

2. The English language is recognised as a second official language.

3. Provision may, however, be made by law for the exclusive use of either of the said languages for any one or more official purposes, either throughout the State or in any part thereof.

[18] As is apparent from the documents before the Court, although Irish is not spoken by the whole Irish population, the policy followed by Irish Governments for many years has been designed not only to maintain but also to promote the use of Irish as a means of expressing national identity and culture. It is for that reason that Irish courses are compulsory for children receiving primary education and optional for those receiving secondary education. The obligation imposed on lecturers in public vocational education schools to have a certain knowledge of the Irish language is one of the measures adopted by the Irish Government in furtherance of that policy.

[19] The EEC Treaty does not prohibit the adoption of a policy for the protection and promotion of a language of a member-State which is both the national language and the first official language. However, the implementation of such a policy must not encroach upon a fundamental freedom such as that of the free movement of workers. Therefore, the requirements deriving from measures intended to implement such a policy must not in any circumstances be disproportionate in relation to the aim pursued and the manner in which they are applied must not bring about discrimination against nationals of other member-States.

[20] The importance of education for the implementation of such a policy must be recognised. Teachers have an essential role to play, not only through the teaching which they provide but also by their participation in the daily life of the school and the privileged relationship which they have with their pupils. In those circumstances, it is not unreasonable to require them to have some knowledge of the first national language.

[21] It follows that the requirement imposed on teachers to have an adequate knowledge of such a language must, provided that the level of knowledge required is not disproportionate in relation to the objective pursued, be regarded as a condition corresponding to the knowledge required by reason of the nature of the post to be filled within the meaning of the last subparagraph of Article 3(1) of Regulation 1612/68.

 Alert

[22] It must also be pointed out that where the national provisions provide for the possibility of exemption from that linguistic requirement where no other fully qualified candidate has applied for the post to be filled, Community law requires that power to grant exemptions to be exercised by the Minister in a non-discriminatory manner.

[23] Moreover, the principle of non-discrimination precludes the imposition of any requirement that the linguistic knowledge in question must have been acquired within the national territory. It also implies that the nationals of other member-States should have an opportunity to re-take the oral examination, in the event of their having previously failed it, when they again apply for a post of assistant lecturer of lecturer.

[24] Accordingly, the reply to the second question must be that a permanent full-time post of lecturer in public vocational education institutions is a post of such a nature as to justify the requirement of linguistic knowledge, within the meaning of the last subparagraph of Article 3(1) of Council Regulation 1612/68, provided that the linguistic requirement in question is imposed as part of a policy for the promotion of the national language which is, at the same time, the first official language and provided that that requirement is applied in a proportionate and non-discriminatory manner. ...

Further Reading

Golynker, Oxana: 'Jobseekers' rights in the European Union: challenges of changing the paradigm of social solidarity' [2005] ELRev 111

8

Sex Discrimination

Topic List

Alex Lawson

Introduction

Sex discrimination requires a small introduction, because it is so different to all the other areas of EU Law. Virtually every other area of substantive law (as opposed to procedural, as with direct effect and Administrative Law) within the EU corpus involves some cross border element somewhere in the analysis. Sex discrimination law does not. The relevant provisions apply within individual states rather than across their borders.

Sex discrimination cases tend to involve factual circumstances that are of limited utility in the application of the principles developed. Simultaneously, however, knowledge of the factual nexus helps in the appreciation of how discrimination occurs in practice. The focus of the ECJ is very much on what actually happens to individuals in the real workplace, rather than abstract concepts of equality. It is therefore necessary to try and keep the principles and the facts separate, whilst ensuring an appreciation of both is maintained.

1 The Meaning of 'Pay': Art 157

The core principle of sex discrimination law has been equality in treatment and pay. The exact definition of 'pay', however, took some time to fully define. It has emerged as 'any consideration, whether in cash or in kind, provided by an employer to employees or to retired employees'. Article 157 (ex Art 141) is the key sex discrimination legislation on this area.

Note that this extract only references the ECJ element of the case, not the House of Lords.

Garland Appellant v British Rail Engineering Ltd. Respondents Case 12/81 [1983] 2 AC 751

Panel: Bosco P, Touffait and O. Due PPC, Pescatore, Lord Mackenzie Stuart, O'Keeffe, Koopmans, Chloros and Grévisse JJ. P. Verloren Van Themaat, Advocate-General

Legislation: Art 157 (ex Art 141)

Facts: Retired male employees were granted travel benefits. Female employees were not. The case was slightly complicated by British Rail Engineering's argument that these benefits were non-contractual and so should not be regarded as pay. The House of Lords referred these issues to the ECJ.

JUDGMENT

3. It was submitted before the House of Lords that that situation was contrary to article 119 and the directives implementing it and the House of Lords therefore referred the following two questions to the court. 1. Where an employer provides (although not bound to do so by contract) special travel facilities for former employees to enjoy after retirement which discriminate against former female employees in the manner described above, is this contrary to: (a) Article 119 of the E.E.C. Treaty? (b) article 1 of

Council Directive (75/117/E.E.C.)? (c) Article 1 of Council Directive (76/207/E.E.C.)? 2. If the answer to questions 1 (a), 1 (b) or 1 (c) is affirmative, is article 119 or either of the said directives directly applicable in member states so as to confer enforceable Community rights upon individuals in the above circumstances?"

Question 1

4. To assist in answering the first question it is first of all necessary to investigate the legal nature of the special travel facilities at issue in this case which the employer grants although not contractually bound to do so.

5. It is important to note in this regard that in paragraph 6 of its judgment of May 25, 1971, in *Defrenne v. Belgian State* (Case 80/70)[1971] E.C.R. 445, 451, the court stated that the concept of pay contained in the second paragraph of article 119 comprises any other consideration, whether in cash or in kind, whether immediate or future, provided that the worker receives it, albeit indirectly, in respect of his employment from his employer.

Alert

6. According to the order making the reference for a preliminary ruling, when male employees of the respondent undertaking retire from their employment on reaching retirement age they continue to be granted special travel facilities for themselves, their wives and their dependent children.

7. A feature of those facilities is that they are granted in kind by the employer to the retired male employee or his dependants directly or indirectly in respect of his employment.

8. Moreover, it appears from a letter sent by British Rail Engineering to the trade unions on December 4, 1975, that the special travel facilities granted after retirement must be considered to be an extension of the facilities granted during the period of employment.

9. It follows from those considerations that rail travel facilities such as those referred to by the House of Lords fulfil the criteria enabling them to be treated as pay within the meaning of article 119 of the E.E.C. Treaty.

10. The argument that the facilities are not related to a contractual obligation is immaterial. The legal nature of the facilities is not important for the purposes of the application of article 119 provided that they are granted in respect of the employment.

11. It follows that where an employer (although not bound to do so by contract) provides special travel facilities for former male employees to enjoy after their retirement this constitutes discrimination within the meaning of article 119 against former female employees who do not receive the same facilities.

12. In view of the interpretation given to article 119 of the E.E.C. Treaty, which by itself answers the question posed by the House of Lords, there is no need to consider points (b) and (c) of question 1 which raise the same question with reference to article 1 of Council Directive (75/117/E.E.C) and of Council Directive (76/207/E.E.C.) .

Question 2

13. Since question 1 (a) has been answered in the affirmative the question arises of the direct applicability of article 119 in the member states and of the rights which individuals may invoke on that basis before national courts.

14. In paragraph 17 of its judgment of March 31, 1981, in *Jenkins v. Kingsgate (Clothing Productions) Ltd.* (Case 96/80)[1981] 1 W.L.R. 972 , 983 the court stated that article 119 of the Treaty applies directly to all forms of discrimination which may be identified solely with the aid of the criteria of equal work and equal pay referred to by the article in question, without national or Community measures being required to define them with greater precision in order to permit of their application.

15. Where a national court is able, using the criteria of equal work and equal pay, without the operation of Community or national measures, to establish that the grant of special transport facilities solely to retired male employees represents discrimination based on difference of sex, the provisions of article 119 of the Treaty apply directly to such a situation.

2   Equal Pay for Work of Equal Value

One of the core principles of sex discrimination law is that where two different jobs involve work of equal value, albeit of a very different nature, they should attract equal (or at least near equal) pay. This was at issue in the following case. Because the principle is rather abstract if taken in isolation from the facts, the extract below draws quite heavily on the factual situation at issue.

Dr. Pamela Enderby v Frenchay Health Authority and Another Case 127/92 [1994] 1 CMLR 8

Panel: Due CJ, Mancini, Moitinho de Almeida and Edward PPC, Joliet, Schockweiler, Grévisse, Zuleeg and Murray JJ. Herr Carl Otto Lenz, Advocate-General

Legislation: Art 157 (ex Art 141, ex Art 119)

Facts: Enderby was a speech therapist who argued that pharmacists and other health professionals of similar seniority were paid more. The case thus hinged on whether or not the different professions were undertaking work of equal value and on how that could be assessed.

JUDGMENT

[1] By order of 30 October 1991, received by the Court of Justice on 17 April 1992, the Court of Appeal of England and Wales, pursuant to Article 177 EEC, referred for a preliminary ruling, questions concerning the interpretation of Article 119 EEC, enshrining the principle of equal pay for men and women.

[2] Those questions were referred in the context of proceedings brought by Dr. Pamela Enderby against the Frenchay Health Authority (hereinafter "FHA") and the Secretary of State for Health concerning the difference in pay between two jobs within the National Health Service (hereinafter "NHS").

[3] The appellant in the main proceedings, who is employed as a speech therapist by the FHA, considers that she is a victim of sex discrimination due to the fact that at her level of seniority within the NHS (Chief III) members of her profession, which is overwhelmingly a female profession, are appreciably less well paid than members of comparable professions in which, at an equivalent professional level, there are more men than women. In 1986, she brought proceedings against her employer before an industrial tribunal, claiming that her annual pay was only £10,106 while that of a principal clinical psychologist and of a Grade III principal pharmacist, jobs which were of equal value to hers, was £12,527 and £14,106 respectively.

[4] Dr. Enderby's claim was dismissed by the industrial tribunal and then, on appeal, by the Employment Appeal Tribunal. The industrial tribunal considered that the differences in pay were the result of structures specific to each profession, and in particular the separate collective bargaining arrangements, which were not discriminatory. The appeal tribunal also considered that the differences were not attributable to discrimination. It held further that it had been established that the state of the employment market played some part in the difference in pay between speech therapists and pharmacists and that that was enough to justify the whole of the difference between those two professions.

[5] On appeal, the Court of Appeal, considering that the outcome of the proceedings depended on the interpretation of Article 119 EEC, decided to refer questions to the Court of Justice for a preliminary ruling. In the statement of facts in its order, the Court of Appeal defined the job of principal speech therapist as "job A" and that of principal pharmacist as "job B," and assumed for the purpose of the present proceedings that those two different jobs were of equal value. It then asked the following questions:

Does the principle of equal pay enshrined in Article 119 EEC require the employer to justify objectively the difference in pay between job A and job B?

If the answer to question 1 is in the affirmative can the employer rely as sufficient justification for the difference in pay upon the fact that the pay of jobs A and B respectively have been determined by different collective bargaining processes which (considered separately) do not discriminate on grounds of sex and do not operate so as to disadvantage women because of their sex?

If the employer is able to establish that at times there are serious shortages of suitable candidates for job B and that he pays the higher remuneration to holders of job B so as to attract them to job B but it can also be established that only part of the difference in pay between job B and job A is due to the need to attract suitable candidates to job B

(a)   is the whole of the difference of pay objectively justified or

(b)   is that part but only that part of the difference which is due to the need to attract suitable candidates to job B objectively justified or

(c)   must the employer equalise the pay of jobs A and B on the ground that he has failed to show that the whole of the difference is objectively justified?

[6] Reference is made to the Report for the Hearing for a fuller account of the facts, the procedure and the written observations submitted to the Court, which are mentioned or discussed hereinafter only in so far as is necessary for the reasoning of the Court.

The first question

[7] In its first question, the Court of Appeal wishes to know whether the principle of equal pay for men and women requires the employer to prove, by providing objective justification, that a difference in pay between two jobs assumed to be of equal value, of which one is carried out almost exclusively by women and the other predominantly by men, does not constitute sex discrimination.

The relevance of the question

[8] The German Government maintains that the Court cannot rule on the question referred without first establishing whether the jobs in question are equivalent. Since, in its view, the jobs of speech therapist and pharmacist are not comparable, there can be no infringement of Article 119 EEC and the pay differentials do not therefore require objective justification.

[9] That proposition cannot be accepted.

[10] The Court has consistently held that Article 177 EEC provides the framework for close co-operation between national courts and the Court of Justice, based on a division of responsibilities between them. Within that framework, it is solely for the national court before which the dispute has been brought, and which must assume the responsibility for the subsequent judicial decision, to determine in the light of the particular circumstances of each case both the need for a preliminary ruling in order to enable it to deliver judgment and the relevance of the question which it submits to the Court: see, in particular, Case *C-67/91, Asociación Española de Banca Privada*.

Accordingly, where the national court's request concerns the interpretation of a provision of Community law, the Court is bound to reply to it, unless it is being asked to rule on a purely hypothetical general problem without having available the information as to fact or law necessary to enable it to give a useful reply to the questions referred to it: see *Case C-83/91, Meilicke*.

[11] In this case, the Court of Appeal, like the tribunals which heard the case below, decided in accordance with the British legislation and with the agreement of the parties to examine the question of the objective justification of the difference in pay before that of the equivalence of the jobs in issue, which may require more complex investigation. It is for that reason that the preliminary questions were based on the assumption that those jobs were of equal value.

[12] Where, as here, the Court receives a request for interpretation of Community law which is not manifestly unrelated to the reality or the subject-matter of the main proceedings, it must reply to that request and is not required to consider the validity of a hypothesis which it is for the referring court to verify subsequently if that should prove to be necessary.

The question referred

[13] It is normally for the person alleging facts in support of a claim to adduce proof of such facts. Thus, in principle, the burden of proving the existence of sex discrimination as to pay lies with the worker who, believing himself to be the victim of such discrimination, brings legal proceedings against his employer with a view to removing the discrimination.

[14] However, it is clear from the case law of the Court that the onus may shift when that is necessary to avoid depriving workers who appear to be the victims of discrimination of any effective means of enforcing the principle of equal pay.

Accordingly, when a measure distinguishing between employees on the basis of their hours of work has in practice an adverse impact on substantially more members of one or other sex, that measure must be regarded as contrary to the objective pursued by Article 119 EEC, unless the employer shows that it is based on objectively justified factors unrelated to any discrimination on grounds of sex: *Case 170/84, Bilka-Kaufhaus, Case C-33/89, Kowalska*, and *C-184/89, Nimz*. Similarly, where an undertaking applies a system of pay which is wholly lacking in transparency, it is for the employer to prove that his practice in the matter of wages is not discriminatory, if a female worker establishes, in relation to a relatively large number of employees, that the average pay for women is less than that for men: *Case 109/88, Danfoss*.

[15] In this case, as both the FHA and the United Kingdom observe, the circumstances are not exactly the same as in the cases just mentioned. First, it is not a question of *de facto* discrimination arising from a particular sort of arrangement such as may apply, for example, in the case of part-time workers. Secondly, there can be no complaint that the employer has applied a system of pay wholly lacking in transparency since the rates of pay of NHS speech therapists and pharmacists are decided by regular collective bargaining processes in which there is no evidence of discrimination as regards either of those two professions.

[16] However, if the pay of speech therapists is significantly lower than that of pharmacists and if the former are almost exclusively women while the latter are predominantly men, there is a *prima facie* case of sex discrimination, at least where the two jobs in question are of equal value and the statistics describing that situation are valid.

[17] It is for the national court to assess whether it may take into account those statistics, that is to say, whether they cover enough individuals, whether they illustrate purely fortuitous or short-term phenomena, and whether, in general, they appear to be significant.

[18] Where there is a *prima facie* case of discrimination, it is for the employer to show that there are objective reasons for the difference in pay. Workers would be unable to enforce the principle of equal pay before national courts if evidence of a *prima facie* case of discrimination did not shift to the employer the onus of showing that the pay differential is not in fact discriminatory: see, by analogy, *Danfoss*.

[19] In these circumstances, the answer to the first question is that, where significant statistics disclose an appreciable difference in pay between two jobs of equal value,

Alert

one of which is carried out almost exclusively by women and the other predominantly by men, Article 119 EEC requires the employer to show that that difference is based on objectively justified factors unrelated to any discrimination on grounds of sex.

The second question

[20] In its second question, the Court of Appeal wishes to know whether the employer can rely as sufficient justification for the difference in pay upon the fact that the rates of pay of the jobs in question were decided by collective bargaining processes which, although carried out by the same parties, are distinct and which, considered separately, have no discriminatory effect.

[21] As is clear from Article 4 of Council Directive 75/117 on the approximation of the laws of the member-States relating to the application of the principle of equal pay for men and women, collective agreements, like laws, regulations or administrative provisions, must observe the principle enshrined in Article 119 EEC.

[22] The fact that the rates of pay at issue are decided by collective bargaining processes conducted separately for each of the two professional groups concerned, without any discriminatory effect within each group, does not preclude a finding of *prima facie* discrimination where the results of those processes show that two groups with the same employer and the same trade union are treated differently. If the employer could rely on the absence of discrimination within each of the collective bargaining processes taken separately as sufficient justification for the difference in pay, he could, as the German Government pointed out, easily circumvent the principle of equal pay by using separate bargaining processes.

[23] Accordingly, the answer to the second question is that the fact that the respective rates of pay of two jobs of equal value, one carried out almost exclusively by women and the other predominantly by men, were arrived at by collective bargaining processes which, although carried out by the same parties, are distinct, and, taken separately, have in themselves no discriminatory effect, is not sufficient objective justification for the difference in pay between those two jobs.

Alert

The third question

[24] In its third question, the Court of Appeal wishes to know to what extent—wholly, in part or not at all—the fact that part of the difference in pay is attributable to a shortage of candidates for one job and to the need to attract them by higher salaries can objectively justify that pay differential.

[25] The Court has consistently held that it is for the national court, which has sole jurisdiction to make findings of fact, to determine whether and to what extent the grounds put forward by an employer to explain the adoption of a pay practice which applies independently of a worker's sex but in fact affects more women than men may be regarded as objectively justified economic grounds: *Case 170/84, Bilka-Kaufhaus,* cited above, and *Case C-184/89, Nimz,* cited above. Those grounds may include, if they can be attributed to the needs and objectives of the undertaking, different criteria such as the worker's flexibility or adaptability to hours and places of work, his training or his length of service: *Case 109/88, Danfoss,* cited above.

[26] The state of the employment market, which may lead an employer to increase the pay of a particular job in order to attract candidates, may constitute an objectively justified economic ground within the meaning of the case law cited above. How it is to be applied in the circumstances of each case depends on the facts and so falls within the jurisdiction of the national court.

[27] If, as the question referred seems to suggest, the national court has been able to determine precisely what proportion of the increase in pay is attributable to market forces, it must necessarily accept that the pay differential is objectively justified to the extent of that proportion. When national authorities have to apply Community law, they must apply the principle of proportionality.

[28] If that is not the case, it is for the national court to assess whether the role of market forces in determining the rate of pay was sufficiently significant to provide objective justification for part or all of the difference.

[29] The answer to the third question therefore is that it is for the national court to determine, if necessary by applying the principle of proportionality, whether and to what extent the shortage of candidates for a job and the need to attract them by higher pay constitutes an objectively justified economic ground for the difference in pay between the jobs in question.

 Alert

3 Discrimination on Grounds of Pregnancy

The ECJ has now consistently held that refusal to employ on the basis of pregnancy is direct discrimination.

Dekker v Stichting Vormingscentrum Voor Jong Volwassenen (VJV-Centrum) Plus Case 177/88 [1992] 1 CMLR 305

Panel: Presiding O. Due, J. C. Moitinho de Almeida, Rodriguez Iglesias and Diez de Velasco PPC, Slynn, Kakouris and Grévisse JJ. M. Darmo, Advocate-General

Legislation: Directive 76/207

Facts: Mrs Dekker applied for a post as a training instructor. As she was pregnant, she informed her potential employers. The selection panel recommended her as the best choice, but she was not employed. The training centre specifically cited her pregnancy as a factor. The ECJ had to consider if this was direct discrimination.

JUDGMENT

1 By judgment of 24 June 1988, which was received at the court on 30 June 1988, the Hoge Raad der Nederlanden referred to the court for a preliminary ruling under article 177 of the E.E.C. Treaty four questions on the interpretation of articles 2 and 3 of the Council Directive of 9 February 1976 (76/207/E.E.C.) on the implementation of the principle of equal treatment for men and women as regards access to employment, vocational training and promotion, and working conditions (Official Journal 1976 No. L 39, p. 40).

2 Those questions arose in the context of a dispute between Mrs. Dekker and the Stichting Vormingscentrum voor Jong Volwassenen (VJV-Centrum) Plus ("the VJV"). In June 1981 Mrs. Dekker applied for the post of instructor at the training centre for young adults run by the VJV. On 15 June 1981, she informed the committee dealing with the applications that she was three months' pregnant. The committee nonetheless put her name forward to the board of management of the VJV as the most suitable candidate for the job. By letter of 10 July 1981, however, the VJV informed Mrs. Dekker that she would not be appointed.

3 In the letter the VJV explained that the reason for the decision was that Mrs. Dekker was already pregnant at the time of lodging her application and that, according to the information it had obtained, the consequence would be that, if the VJV were to employ her, its insurer, the Risicofonds Sociale Voorzieningen Bijzonder Onderwijs (Assurance Fund for the provision of social benefits in special education; hereinafter referred to as "the Risicofonds") would not reimburse the daily benefits that the VJV would be obliged to pay her during her maternity leave. As a result, the VJV would be financially unable to employ a replacement during Mrs. Dekker's absence and would thus be short staffed.

4 It is apparent from the documents before the court that under article 6 of the Ziekengeldreglement (the internal rules of the Risicofonds governing daily sickness benefits) the board of management of the Risicofonds is empowered to refuse to reimburse to a member (the employer) all or part of the daily benefits in the event that an insured person (the employee) becomes unable to perform his or her duties within six months of commencement of the insurance if, at the time when that insurance took effect, it was to be anticipated from the state of health of the person concerned that such incapacity would supervene within that period. Unlike article 44(1)(b) of the Ziektewet (the Netherlands Law on sickness insurance), which lays down the insurance scheme generally applicable to private sector employees, the Ziekengeldreglement, which alone applies to Mrs. Dekker, contains no derogation for pregnancy from the rule permitting reimbursement of the daily benefits to be refused in cases of "foreseeable sickness."

5 The Arrondissementsrechtbank (District Court) Haarlem and the Gerechtshof (Regional Court of Appeal), in turn, dismissed Mrs. Dekker's applications for an order requiring the VJV to pay her damages for her financial loss, whereupon she appealed to the Hoge Raad der Nederlanden (Supreme Court of the Netherlands).

6 Taking the view that the appeal raised problems as to the interpretation of Council Directive (76/207/E.E.C.), the Hoge Raad der Nederlanden decided to refer the following questions to the court for a preliminary ruling:

"1. Is an employer directly or indirectly in breach of the principle of equal treatment laid down in articles 2(1) and 3(1) of the Council Directive of 9 February 1976 (76/207/E.E.C.) on the implementation of the principle of equal treatment for men and women as regards access to employment, vocational training and promotion, and working conditions if he refuses to enter into a contract of employment with a candidate, found by him to be suitable, because of the adverse consequences for him which are to be anticipated owing to the fact that the candidate was pregnant when she applied for the post, in conjunction with rules concerning unfitness for work laid down by a public authority under which inability to work in connection with pregnancy and confinement is assimilated to inability to work on account of sickness?

"2. Does it make any difference that there were no male candidates?

"3. Is it compatible with articles 2 and 3: (a) that, if a breach of the principle that the rejected candidate must be accorded equal treatment is established, fault on the part of the employer is also required before a claim based on that breach such as the present can be upheld; or (b) that if such a breach is established, the employer for his part can still plead justification, even if none of the cases provided for in article 2(2) to (4) applies?

"4. If fault as referred to in question 3 above may be required or grounds of justification may be pleaded, is it then sufficient, in order for there to be absence of fault or for a ground of justification to exist, that the employer runs the risk referred to in the summary of the facts, or must articles 2 and 3 be interpreted as meaning that he must bear those risks, unless he has satisfied himself beyond all doubt that the benefit on account of unfitness for work will be refused or that posts will be lost, and he has done everything possible to prevent that from happening?"

7 Reference is made to the report for the hearing for a fuller account of the facts of the case, the course of the procedure and the written observations submitted to the court, which are mentioned or discussed hereinafter only in so far as is necessary for the reasoning of the court.

First question

8 It should be noted at the outset that the purpose of the Directive, according to article 1(1), is to put into effect in the member states the principle of equal treatment for men and women as regards access to employment, vocational training and promotion, and working conditions.

9 Article 2(1) of the Directive provides:

"the principle of equal treatment shall mean that there shall be no discrimination whatsoever on grounds of sex either directly or indirectly by reference in particular to marital or family status."

Under article 3(1) :

"Application of the principle of equal treatment means that there shall be no discrimination whatsoever on grounds of sex in the conditions, including selection criteria, for access to all jobs or posts..."

10 Consideration must be given to the question whether a refusal of employment in the circumstances to which the national court has referred may be regarded as direct discrimination on the ground of sex for the purposes of the Directive. The answer

depends on whether the fundamental reason for the refusal of employment is one which applies without distinction to workers of either sex or, conversely, whether it applies exclusively to one sex.

11 The reason given by the employer for refusing to appoint Mrs. Dekker is basically that it could not have obtained reimbursement from the Risicofonds of the daily benefits which it would have had to pay her for the duration of her absence due to pregnancy, and yet at the same time it would have been obliged to employ a replacement. That situation arises because, on the one hand, the national scheme in question assimilates pregnancy to sickness and, on the other, the Ziekengeldreglement contains no provision excluding pregnancy from the cases in which the Risicofonds is entitled to refuse reimbursement of the daily benefits.

12 In that regard it should be observed that only women can be refused employment on the ground of pregnancy and such a refusal therefore constitutes direct discrimination on the ground of sex. A refusal of employment on account of the financial consequences of absence due to pregnancy must be regarded as based, essentially, on the fact of pregnancy. Such discrimination cannot be justified on grounds relating to the financial loss which an employer who appointed a pregnant woman would suffer for the duration of her maternity leave.

 Alert

13 In any event, the fact that pregnancy is assimilated to sickness and that the respective provisions of the Ziektewet and the Ziekengeldreglement governing reimbursement of the daily benefits payable in connection with pregnancy are not the same cannot be regarded as evidence of discrimination on the ground of sex within the meaning of the Directive. Lastly, in so far as an employer's refusal of employment based on the financial consequences of absence due to pregnancy constitutes direct discrimination, it is not necessary to consider whether national provisions such as those mentioned above exert such pressure on the employer that they prompt him to refuse to appoint a pregnant woman, thereby leading to discrimination within the meaning of the Directive.

14 It follows from the foregoing that the answer to be given to the first question is that an employer is in direct contravention of the principle of equal treatment embodied in articles 2(1) and 3(1) of Council Directive (76/207/E.E.C.) on the implementation of the principle of equal treatment for men and women as regards access to employment, vocational training and promotion, and working conditions if he refuses to enter into a contract of employment with a female candidate whom he considers to be suitable for the job where such refusal is based on the possible adverse consequences for him of employing a pregnant woman, owing to rules on unfitness for work adopted by the public authorities which assimilate inability to work on account of pregnancy and confinement to inability to work on account of illness.

 Alert

Second question

15 In its second question the Hoge Raad asks whether the fact that there was no male candidate for the job is liable to alter the answer to the first question.

16 The VJV contends that the second question must be answered in the affirmative, because what is involved is not the discriminatory effect of an abstract measure but a concrete decision by an employer not to engage a specific candidate. When an employer chooses from among exclusively female candidates, his choice cannot be attributable to discrimination on the ground of sex, because in such a case the employer is guided by other considerations of a financial or administrative nature.

17 It should be stressed that the reply to the question whether the refusal to employ a woman constitutes direct or indirect discrimination depends on the reason for that refusal. If that reason is to be found in the fact that the person concerned is pregnant, then the decision is directly linked to the sex of the candidate. In those circumstances the absence of male candidates cannot affect the answer to the first question.

 Alert

18 The answer to be given to the second question must therefore be that the fact that no man applied for the job does not alter the answer to the first question.

Third question

19 The third question relates to whether it is contrary to articles 2 and 3 of the Directive for a legal action in damages based on breach of the principle of equal treatment to be capable of succeeding only if it is also proved that the employer is at fault and cannot avail himself of any ground exempting him from liability.

20 Mrs. Dekker, the Netherlands Government and the United Kingdom all take the view that, once an infringement of the principle of equal treatment is established, that infringement must be sufficient to make the employer liable.

21 For its part, the VJV notes that the distinction drawn in the two limbs of the third question between fault attributable to the employer and the possible absence of any ground exempting him from liability is partly linked to the national law applicable to the main proceedings, which provides different legal consequences, according to the case. The VJV claims that the Directive allows an answer to be given only to the question whether an infringement of the principle of equal treatment may be justified in any given case.

22 It must be observed in this regard that article 2(2), (3) and (4) of the Directive provide for exceptions to the principle of equal treatment set out in article 2(1), but that the Directive does not make liability on the part of the person guilty of discrimination conditional in any way on proof of fault or on the absence of any ground discharging such liability.

23 Article 6 of the Directive recognises the existence of rights vesting in the victims of discrimination which can be pleaded in legal proceedings. Although full implementation of the Directive does not require any specific form of sanction for unlawful discrimination, it does entail that that sanction be such as to guarantee real and effective protection: *von Colson and Kamann v. Land Nordrhein-Westfalen (Case 14/83)* [1984] E.C.R. 1891, para. 23. It must, furthermore, have a real deterrent effect on the employer.

24 It must be observed that, if the employer's liability for infringement of the principle of equal treatment were made subject to proof of a fault attributable to him and also to there being no ground of exemption recognised by the applicable national law, the practical effect of those principles would be weakened considerably.

25 It follows that when the sanction chosen by the member state is contained within the rules governing an employer's civil liability, any breach of the prohibition of discrimination must, in itself, be sufficient to make the employer liable, without there being any possibility of invoking the grounds of exemption provided by national law.

26 Accordingly, the answer must be that, although the Directive gives the member states, in penalising infringement of the prohibition of discrimination, freedom to choose between the various solutions appropriate for achieving its purpose, it nevertheless requires that, where a member state opts for a sanction forming part of the rules on civil liability, any infringement of the prohibition of discrimination suffices in itself to make the person guilty of it fully liable, and no regard may be had to the grounds of exemption envisaged by national law.

 Alert

Fourth question

27 In view of the answer to the third question, there is no need to give a ruling on the fourth question.

Mary Brown v Rentokil Limited Case 394/96 [1998] 2 CMLR 1049

Panel: Gulmann acting P, Ragnemalm, Wathelet and Schintgen PPC, Mancini, Kapteyn (Rapporteur), Murray, Edward, Puissochet, Jann and Sevón JJ. Mr D. Ruiz-Jarabo Colomer, Advocate-General

Legislation: Directive 76/207

Facts: The case revolved around the issue of a female employee who was absent from work due to a pregnancy related illness. It was clear she would be protected from dismissal if this was to occur during her maternity leave. However, in *Larsson v Fotex Supermarked* Case 400/95 [1997] 2 CMLR 915, it had been decided that such protection did not begin until maternity leave itself began. So illness between conception and maternity leave could lead to dismissal. The instant case reversed this odd decision.

JUDGMENT
[1] By order of 28 November 1996, received at the Court Registry on 9 December 1996, the House of Lords referred to the Court for a preliminary ruling under Article 177 E.C., two questions on the interpretation of Articles 2(1) and 5(1) of Council Directive 76/207 on the implementation of the principle of equal treatment for men and women as regards access to employment, vocational training and promotion, and working conditions.

[2] Those questions have been raised in proceedings brought by Mary Brown against Rentokil Ltd (hereinafter "Rentokil") in connection with her dismissal whilst pregnant.

[3] According to the order for reference, Mrs Brown was employed by Rentokil as a driver. Her job was mainly to transport and change "Sanitact" units in shops and other centres. In her view, it was heavy work.

[4] In August 1990, Mrs Brown informed Rentokil that she was pregnant. Thereafter she had difficulties associated with the pregnancy. From 16 August 1990 onwards, she submitted a succession of four-week certificates mentioning various pregnancy-related disorders. She did not work again after mid-August 1990.

[5] Rentokil's contracts of employment included a clause stipulating that, if an employee was absent because of sickness for more than 26 weeks continuously, he or she would be dismissed.

[6] On 9 November 1990, Rentokil's representatives told Mrs Brown that half of the 26-week period had run and that her employment would end on 8 February 1991 if, following an independent medical examination, she had not returned to work by then. A letter to the same effect was sent to her on that date.

[7] Mrs Brown did not go back to work following that letter. The parties agree that there was never any question of her being able to return to work before the end of the 26-week period. By letter of 30 January 1991, which took effect on 8 February 1991, she was accordingly dismissed while pregnant. Her child was born on 22 March 1991. ...

[13] Mrs Brown appealed to the House of Lords, which referred the following questions to the Court for a preliminary ruling:

1.(a) Is it contrary to Articles 2(1) and 5(1) of Directive 76/207 of the Council of the European Communities (the Equal Treatment Directive) to dismiss a female employee, at any time during her pregnancy, as a result of absence through illness arising from that pregnancy?

(b) Does it make any difference to the answer given to Question 1(a) that the employee was dismissed in pursuance of a contractual provision entitling the employer to dismiss employees, irrespective of gender, after a stipulated number of weeks of continued absence?

2. (a) Is it contrary to Articles 2(1) and 5(1) of the Equal Treatment Directive to dismiss a female employee as a result of absence through illness arising from pregnancy who does not qualify for the right to absent herself from work on account of pregnancy or childbirth for the period specified by national law because she has not been employed for the period imposed by national law, where dismissal takes place during that period?

(b) Does it make any difference to the answer given to Question 2(a) that the employee was dismissed in pursuance of a contractual provision entitling the employer to dismiss employees, irrespective of gender, after a stipulated number of weeks of continued absence?

The first part of the first question

[14] It should be noted at the outset that the purpose of Directive 76/207, according to Article 1(1), is to put into effect in the Member States the principle of equal treatment for men and women as regards access to employment, vocational training and promotion, and working conditions.

[15] Article 2(1) of the Directive provides that:

... the principle of equal treatment shall mean that there shall be no discrimination whatsoever on grounds of sex either directly or indirectly by reference in particular to marital or family status.

According to Article 5(1) of the Directive:

[a]pplication of the principle of equal treatment with regard to working conditions, including the conditions governing dismissal, means that men and women shall be guaranteed the same conditions without discrimination on grounds of sex.

[16] According to settled case law of the Court of Justice, the dismissal of a female worker on account of pregnancy, or essentially on account of pregnancy, can affect only women and therefore constitutes direct discrimination on grounds of sex (see *Case C-177/88, Dekker v Stichting Vormingscentrum voor Jong Volwassenen (Vjv-Centrum) Plus; Hertz; Case C-421/92, Habermann-Beltermann v Arbeiterwohlfahrt Bezirksverband* and *Case C-32/93, Webb v EMO Air Cargo*).

[17] As the Court pointed out in paragraph [20] of its judgment in *Webb*, by reserving to Member States the right to retain or introduce provisions which are intended to protect women in connection with "pregnancy and maternity", Article 2(3) of Directive 76/207 recognises the legitimacy, in terms of the principle of equal treatment, first, of protecting a woman's biological condition during and after pregnancy and, second, of protecting the special relationship between a woman and her child over the period which follows pregnancy and childbirth.

[18] It was precisely in view of the harmful effects which the risk of dismissal may have on the physical and mental state of women who are pregnant, women who have recently given birth or women who are breastfeeding, including the particularly serious risk that pregnant women may be prompted voluntarily to terminate their pregnancy, that the Community legislature, pursuant to Article 10 of Council Directive 92/85 on the introduction of measures to encourage improvements in the safety and health at work of pregnant workers and workers who have recently given birth or are breastfeeding (tenth individual Directive adopted within the meaning of Article 16(1) of Directive 89/391), which was to be transposed into the laws of the Member States no later than two years after its adoption, provided for special protection to be given to women, by prohibiting dismissal during the period from the beginning of their pregnancy to the end of their maternity leave. Article 10 of Directive 92/85 provides that there is to be no exception to, or derogation from, the prohibition of dismissal of pregnant women during that period, save in exceptional cases not connected with their condition (see, in this regard, paragraphs [21] and [22] of the judgment in *Webb*).

[19] In replying to the first part of the first question, which concerns Directive 76/207, account must be taken of that general context.

[20] At the outset, it is clear from the documents before the Court that the question concerns the dismissal of a female worker during her pregnancy as a result of absences through incapacity for work arising from her pregnant condition. As Rentokil points out, the cause of Mrs Brown's dismissal lies in the fact that she was ill during her pregnancy to such an extent that she was unfit for work for 26 weeks. It is common ground that her illness was attributable to her pregnancy.

[21] However, dismissal of a woman during pregnancy cannot be based on her inability, as a result of her condition, to perform the duties which she is contractually bound to carry out. If such an interpretation were adopted, the protection afforded by Community law to a woman during pregnancy would be available only to pregnant women who were able to comply with the conditions of their employment contracts, with the result that the provisions of Directive 76/207 would be rendered ineffective.

[22] Although pregnancy is not in any way comparable to a pathological condition, the fact remains, as the Advocate General stresses in point 56 of his Opinion, that pregnancy is a period during which disorders and complications may arise compelling a woman to undergo strict medical supervision and, in some cases, to rest absolutely for all or part of her pregnancy. Those disorders and complications, which may cause incapacity for work, form part of the risks inherent in the condition of pregnancy and are thus a specific feature of that condition.

[23] In paragraph 15 of its judgment in *Hertz*, cited above, the Court, on the basis of Article 2(3) of Directive 76/207, also pointed out that that directive admits of national provisions guaranteeing women specific rights on account of pregnancy and maternity. It concluded that, during the maternity leave accorded to her under national law, a woman is protected against dismissal on the grounds of her absence.

[24] Although, under Article 2(3) of Directive 76/207, such protection against dismissal must be afforded to women during maternity leave, the principle of non-discrimination, for its part, requires similar protection throughout the period of pregnancy. Finally, as is clear from paragraph [22] of this judgment, dismissal of a female worker during pregnancy for absences due to incapacity for work resulting from her pregnancy is linked to the occurrence of risks inherent in pregnancy and must therefore be regarded as essentially based on the fact of pregnancy. Such a dismissal can affect only women and therefore constitutes direct discrimination on grounds of sex.

[25] It follows that Articles 2(1) and 5(1) of Directive 76/207 preclude dismissal of a female worker at any time during her pregnancy for absences due to incapacity for work caused by an illness resulting from that pregnancy.

[26] However, where pathological conditions caused by pregnancy or childbirth arise after the end of maternity leave, they are covered by the general rules applicable in the event of illness. In such circumstances, the sole question is whether a female worker's absences, following maternity leave, caused by her incapacity for work brought on by such disorders, are treated in the same way as a male worker's absences, of the same

duration, caused by incapacity for work; if they are, there is no discrimination on grounds of sex.

[27] It is also clear from all the foregoing considerations that, contrary to the Court's ruling in *Case C-400/95, Larsson v. Føtex Supermarked,* where a woman is absent owing to illness resulting from pregnancy or childbirth, and that illness arose during pregnancy and persisted during and after maternity leave, her absence not only during maternity leave but also during the period extending from the start of her pregnancy to the start of her maternity leave cannot be taken into account for computation of the period justifying her dismissal under national law. As to her absence after maternity leave, this may be taken into account under the same conditions as a man's absence, of the same duration, through incapacity for work.

[28] The answer to the first part of the first question must therefore be that Articles 2(1) and 5(1) of Directive 76/207 preclude dismissal of a female worker at any time during her pregnancy for absences due to incapacity for work caused by illness resulting from that pregnancy.

The second part of the first question

[29] The second part of the first question concerns a contractual term providing that an employer may dismiss workers of either sex after a stipulated number of weeks of continuous absence.

[30] It is well settled that discrimination involves the application of different rules to comparable situations or the application of the same rule to different situations (see, in particular, *Case C-342/93, Gillespie and Others v. Northern Health and Social Services Board and Others).*

[31] Where it is relied on to dismiss a pregnant worker because of absences due to incapacity for work resulting from her pregnancy, such a contractual term, applying both to men and to women, is applied in the same way to different situations since, as is clear from the answer given to the first part of the first question, the situation of a pregnant worker who is unfit for work as a result of disorders associated with her pregnancy cannot be considered to be the same as that of a male worker who is ill and absent through incapacity for work for the same length of time.

[32] Consequently, application of that contractual term in circumstances such as the present constitutes direct discrimination on grounds of sex.

[33] The answer to the second part of the first question must therefore be that the fact that a female worker has been dismissed during her pregnancy on the basis of a contractual term providing that the employer may dismiss employees of either sex after a stipulated number of weeks of continuous absence cannot affect the answer given to the first part of the first question.

The second question

[34] In view of the answer given to the first question, it is unnecessary to answer the second question.

3.1 Pregnancy and Fixed and Open-ended Contracts of Employment

Previous case law (*Webb v. EMO Air Cargo (UK) Ltd* Case 32/93 [1994] 2 CMLR 729) had suggested that fixed term contracts of employment for female workers would essentially be worthless if the employee was unable to fulfil much of the fixed term due to pregnancy. This appears to be a sensible decision, but the simple fact is that none of the extant pieces of legislation made this distinction. It was simply suggested by the ECJ out of the blue. The following case resolved this aberrant decision and also addressed the question of whether there was a duty to tell prospective employers about pregnancy.

Tele Danmark A/S v Handels- og Kontorfunktion ÆRernes Forbund I Danmark (acting on behalf of Brandt-Nielsen) Case 109/00 [2002] 1 CMLR 5

Panel: La Pergola PC, Wathelet (Rapporteur), Jann, Sevón and Timmermans, JJ.

Legislation: Directives 76/207 and 92/85

Facts: Brandt-Nielsen, a female employee was recruited for a fixed period. She was pregnant at the time and knew so, but did not inform the employers. Because of the pregnancy, she was unable to fulfil much of the contract period. The main question for the ECJ was whether there was a duty to inform the employers about her pregnancy and whether failure to do so could lead to legitimate dismissal.

JUDGMENT

1 By order of 21 March 2000, received at the Court on 23 March 2000, the Højesteret (Supreme Court, Denmark) referred to the Court for a preliminary ruling under Article 234 E.C. two questions on the interpretation of Article 5(1) of Council Directive 76/207 on the implementation of the principle of equal treatment for men and women as regards access to employment, vocational training and promotion, and working conditions and Article 10 of Council Directive 92/85 on the introduction of measures to encourage improvements in the safety and health at work of pregnant workers and workers who have recently given birth or are breastfeeding (tenth individual Directive within the meaning of Article 16(1) of Directive 89/391).

2 The two questions have been raised in proceedings between Tele Danmark A/S, a telephone undertaking, and Handels-og Kontorfunktionærernes Forbund i Danmark (Danish Union of Commercial and Office Employees, hereinafter "HK"), acting on behalf of Ms Brandt-Nielsen, following her dismissal by Tele Danmark.

Legal background

Community legislation

3 Directive 76/207 is intended to implement the principle of equal treatment for men and women as regards access to employment, including promotion, and to professional training, and working conditions.

4 Article 3(1) of Directive 76/207 provides:

Application of the principle of equal treatment means that there shall be no discrimination whatsoever on grounds of sex in the conditions, including selection criteria, for access to all jobs or posts, whatever the sector or branch of activity, and to all levels of the occupational hierarchy.

5 Article 5(1) of Directive 76/207 states:

Application of the principle of equal treatment with regard to working conditions, including the conditions governing dismissal, means that men and women shall be guaranteed the same conditions without discrimination on grounds of sex.

6 Directive 92/85 is intended in particular, as stated in the 15th recital in its preamble, to protect pregnant workers, workers who have recently given birth and workers who are breastfeeding against the risk of dismissal for reasons associated with their condition, which could have harmful effects on their physical and mental state.

7 Article 10(1) of Directive 92/85 thus provides:

Member States shall take the necessary measures to prohibit the dismissal of workers … during the period from the beginning of their pregnancy to the end of the maternity leave … save in exceptional cases not connected with their condition which are permitted under national legislation and/or practice and, where applicable, provided that the competent authority has given its consent.

8 The 14th recital in the preamble to Directive 92/85 states that, in view of their vulnerability, it is necessary for pregnant workers, workers who have recently given birth or who are breastfeeding to be allowed maternity leave. Such a right is provided for in Article 8 of that directive, which reads as follows:

1. Member States shall take the necessary measures to ensure that workers within the meaning of Article 2 are entitled to a continuous period of maternity leave of at least 14 weeks allocated before and/or after confinement in accordance with national legislation and/or practice.

2. The maternity leave stipulated in paragraph 1 must include compulsory maternity leave of at least two weeks allocated before and/or after confinement in accordance with national legislation and/or practice.

National legislation

[The court set out the national law and continued]

The main proceedings and the questions referred for a preliminary ruling

11 In June 1995, Ms Brandt-Nielsen was recruited by Tele Danmark for a period of six months from 1 July 1995, to work in its customer service department for mobile telephones. It was agreed between the parties at the recruitment interview that Ms Brandt-Nielsen would have to follow a training course during the first two months of her contract.

12 In August 1995, Ms Brandt-Nielsen informed Tele Danmark that she was pregnant and expected to give birth in early November. Shortly afterwards, on 23 August 1995, she was dismissed with effect from 30 September, on the ground that she had not informed Tele Danmark that she was pregnant when she was recruited. She worked for the whole of September.

13 Under the applicable collective agreement, Ms Brandt-Nielsen would have been entitled to paid maternity leave starting eight weeks before the expected date of giving birth. In the present case, that period should have started on 11 September 1995.

14 On 4 March 1996, HK, acting on behalf of Ms Brandt-Nielsen, brought proceedings against Tele Danmark before the Retten i Århus (District Court, Århus) for compensation, on the ground that her dismissal by Tele Danmark was contrary to Paragraph 9 of the Equal Treatment Law.

15 The Retten i Århus, by judgment of 14 January 1997, dismissed the action on the ground that Ms Brandt-Nielsen, who had been recruited for a six-month period, had failed to state that she was pregnant at the recruitment interview, although she was expected to give birth during the fifth month of the contract of employment.

16 By judgment of 15 April 1999, the Vestre Landsret (Western Regional Court), hearing Ms Brandt-Nielsen's appeal, ruled in her favour on the ground that it was not disputed that the dismissal was linked to her pregnancy.

17 Tele Danmark appealed to the Højesteret against that decision, arguing that the prohibition under Community law of dismissing a pregnant worker did not apply to a worker, recruited on a temporary basis, who, despite knowing that she was pregnant when the contract of employment was concluded, failed to inform the employer of this, and because of her right to maternity leave was unable, for a substantial part of the duration of that contract, to perform the work for which she had been recruited.

18 Those were the circumstances in which the Højesteret stayed the proceedings and referred the following questions to the Court for a preliminary ruling:

(1) Do Article 5(1) of Council Directive 76/207 on the implementation of the principle of equal treatment for men and women as regards access to employment, vocational training and promotion, and working conditions and/or Article 10 of Council Directive 92/85 on the introduction of measures to encourage improvements in the safety and health at work of pregnant workers and workers who have recently given birth or are breastfeeding, or other provisions in those directives or elsewhere in Community law preclude a worker from being dismissed on the ground of pregnancy in the case where:

(i) the woman in question was recruited as a temporary worker for a limited period;

(ii) when she entered into the contract of employment, the worker knew that she was pregnant but did not inform the employer of that fact; and

(iii) her pregnancy meant that the worker was unable to work for a significant portion of her period of employment?

(2) Does the fact that the employment occurs in a very large undertaking and that that undertaking frequently uses temporary workers have any bearing on the answer to Question 1?

The first question

19 By its first question the Højesteret asks essentially whether Article 5(1) of Directive 76/207 and Article 10 of Directive 92/85 must be interpreted as precluding a worker from being dismissed on the ground of pregnancy where she was recruited for a fixed period, she failed to inform the employer that she was pregnant even though she was aware of this when the contract of employment was concluded, and because of her pregnancy she was unable to work during a substantial part of the term of that contract.

20 Tele Danmark submits that the prohibition under Directives 76/207 and 92/85 of dismissing a worker who is pregnant does not apply in the circumstances of the present case. It was not in fact the pregnancy itself which was the determining reason for Ms Brandt-Nielsen's dismissal but the fact that she was unable to perform a substantial part of the contract. Moreover, the fact that she failed to inform the employer of her pregnancy, despite knowing that she would be unable to work during a substantial part of the term of the contract owing to her pregnancy, constituted a breach of the duty of good faith required in relations between employees and employers, capable in itself of justifying dismissal.

21 Tele Danmark says that it is only where the contract has been concluded for an indefinite period that refusing to employ a pregnant woman or dismissing her contravenes Community law. In such an employment relationship, it must be presumed that the worker's obligations will continue beyond the maternity leave, so that observance of the principle of equal treatment leads to a fair result.

22 Ms Brandt-Nielsen, the Commission and the EFTA Surveillance Authority submit, on the other hand, that neither directives 76/207 and 92/85 nor the case law of the Court makes a distinction according to whether the contract under which the worker has been recruited is for a fixed or an indefinite period.

23 They submit that in the present case both Directive 76/207 and Directive 92/85 preclude the dismissal of Ms Brandt-Nielsen, since the reason for dismissal was clearly her pregnancy. According to the Court's case law, neither financial loss incurred by the employer nor the requirements of the proper functioning of his undertaking can justify the dismissal of a pregnant worker, as the employer has to assume the risk of the economic and organisation consequences of the pregnancy of employees.

 **Alert**

24 As to the circumstances that Ms Brandt-Nielsen failed to state that she was pregnant when she was recruited, the Commission submits that a worker is not obliged to inform her employer of her condition, since the employer is not entitled to take it into account on recruitment. The EFTA Surveillance Authority adds that, if such an obligation to inform the employer were accepted, it could render ineffective the protection of pregnant workers established by Article 10 of Directive 92/85, even though the Community legislature intended such protection to be especially high.

 **Alert**

25 As the Court has held on several occasions, the dismissal of a female worker on account of pregnancy constitutes direct discrimination on grounds of sex, contrary to Article 5(1) of Directive 76/207.

26 It was also in view of the risk that a possible dismissal may pose for the physical and mental state of pregnant workers, workers who have recently given birth or those who are breastfeeding, including the particularly serious risk that they may be encouraged to have abortions, that the Community legislature, in Article 10 of Directive 92/85, laid down special protection for those workers by prohibiting dismissal during the period from the start of pregnancy to the end of maternity leave.

27 During that period, Article 10 of Directive 92/85 does not provide for any exception to, or derogation from, the prohibition of dismissing pregnant workers, save in exceptional cases not connected with their condition where the employer justifies the dismissal in writing.

28 The Court has held, moreover, that a refusal to employ a woman on account of her pregnancy cannot be justified on grounds relating to the financial loss which an employer who appointed a pregnant woman would suffer for the duration of her maternity leave, and that the same conclusion must be drawn as regards the financial loss caused by the fact that the woman appointed cannot be employed in the post concerned for the duration of her pregnancy.

Alert

29 In paragraph 26 of *Webb*, the Court also held that, while the availability of an employee is necessarily, for the employer, a precondition for the proper performance of the employment contract, the protection afforded by Community law to a woman during pregnancy and after childbirth cannot be dependent on whether her presence at work during the period corresponding to maternity leave is essential to the proper functioning of the undertaking in which she is employed. A contrary interpretation would render ineffective the provisions of Directive 76/207.

30 Such an interpretation cannot be altered by the fact that the contract of employment was concluded for a fixed term.

31 Since the dismissal of a worker on account of pregnancy constitutes direct discrimination on grounds of sex, whatever the nature and extent of the economic loss incurred by the employer as a result of her absence because of pregnancy, whether the contract of employment was concluded for a fixed or an indefinite period has no bearing on the discriminatory character of the dismissal. In either case the employee's inability to perform her contract of employment is due to pregnancy.

Alert

32 Moreover, the duration of an employment relationship is a particularly uncertain element of the relationship in that, even if the worker is recruited under a fixed-term contract, such a relationship may be for a longer or shorter period, and is moreover liable to be renewed or extended.

33 Finally, Directives 76/207 and 92/85 do not make any distinction, as regards the scope of the principle of equal treatment for men and women, according to the duration of the employment relationship in question. Had the Community legislature wished to exclude fixed-term contracts, which represent a substantial proportion of

employment relationships, from the scope of those directives, it would have done so expressly.

The second question

35 By its second question the Højesteret asks whether the fact that the worker has been recruited by a very large undertaking which frequently uses temporary workers is of relevance to the interpretation of Article 5(1) of Directive 76/207 and Article 10 of Directive 92/85.

36 The parties to the main proceedings agree with the Commission and the EFTA Surveillance Authority that this question should be answered in the negative.

37 It suffices to observe that Directives 76/207 and 92/85 do not distinguish, as regards the scope of the prohibitions they lay down and the rights they guarantee, according to the size of the undertaking concerned.

38 As to the fact that the employer makes considerable use of fixed-term contracts, it must be noted, as appears from paragraphs 30 to 33 above, that the duration of the employment relationship has no bearing on the extent of the protection guaranteed to pregnant workers by Community law.

39 The answer to the second question must therefore be that the fact that the worker has been recruited by a very large undertaking which employs temporary workers frequently is of no relevance to the interpretation of Article 5(1) of Directive 76/207 and Article 10 of Directive 92/85.

 Alert

Further Reading

Caracciolo Di Torella, Eugenia; Masselot, Annick: 'Pregnancy, maternity and the organisation of family life: an attempt to classify the case law of the Court of Justice' [2001] EL Rev 239

Stott, David: 'What price certainty?' [2002] ELRev 351

Notes

Notes

Notes

Notes

Notes

Notes

Notes